The First Amendment and the Media in the Court of Public Opinion

In light of recent frustrations with the press over its increasingly sensationalistic coverage of the news, no liberty may be more vulnerable to the vagaries of the current political climate than the freedom of the press. By considering public opinion data from two original surveys (in 1997 and 1999) on free press rights against the backdrop of modern First Amendment jurisprudence, the authors offer new and original insights into the nature of popular support for these rights. Their findings are as comforting as they are counterintuitive: Public support for the constitutional right to a free press remains as strong as ever, even as its most visible practitioners find themselves increasingly under siege.

In offering this argument, Yalof and Dautrich stake a position in an age-old debate over the true value and worth of public opinion. Their findings endorse the notion of a "rational" public as well as the strength of press freedoms in our society.

David A. Yalof is an assistant professor of political science at the University of Connecticut. His first book, *Pursuit of Justices: Presidential Politics and the Selection of Supreme Court Nominees* (1999), won the American Political Science Association's Richard E. Neustadt Prize as the best book on the presidency in 1999.

Kenneth Dautrich is an associate professor of political science and director of the Institute of Public Affairs at the University of Connecticut. He is the author of *How the News Media Fail American Voters* (1999).

The First Amendment and the Media in the Court of Public Opinion

DAVID A. YALOF

University of Connecticut

KENNETH DAUTRICH

University of Connecticut

CAMBRIDGE
UNIVERSITY PRESS

PUBLISHED BY THE PRESS SYNDICATE OF THE UNIVERSITY OF CAMBRIDGE
The Pitt Building, Trumpington Street, Cambridge, United Kingdom

CAMBRIDGE UNIVERSITY PRESS
The Edinburgh Building, Cambridge CB2 2RU, UK
40 West 20th Street, New York, NY 10011-4211, USA
10 Stamford Road, Oakleigh, VIC 3166, Australia
Ruiz de Alarcón 13, 28014 Madrid, Spain
Dock House, The Waterfront, Cape Town 8001, South Africa

http://www.cambridge.org

First published 2002

Printed in the United States of America

Typeface Sabon 10/12 pt.   *System* QuarkXPress [BTS]

A catalog record for this book is available from the British Library.

Library of Congress Cataloging in Publication Data
Yalof, David Alistair.
The First Amendment and the media in the court of public opinion / David Yalof,
Kenneth Dautrich.
p. cm.
Includes bibliographical references and index.
ISBN 0-521-80466-3 – ISBN 0-521-01181-7 (pbk.)
1. Freedom of the press – United States. 2. Freedom of the press – United States –
Public opinion. 3. Public opinion – United States. I. Dautrich, Kenneth. II. Title.
PN4738 .Y35 2001
323.44′5′0973–dc21   2001025913

ISBN 0 521 80466 3 hardback
ISBN 0 521 01181 7 paperback

Contents

Tables and Figures

TABLES

FIGURES

Preface and Acknowledgments

In a democracy, civil liberties are a precious commodity. Accordingly, we often worry that those liberties have become fragile or increasingly vulnerable to assault. Are such fears well founded? In light of recent frustrations with the press over its increasingly sensationalized coverage of the news, no liberty may be more susceptible to the vagaries of the current political climate than is the constitutional guarantee of a "freedom of the press," which in today's society encompasses print and electronic media alike. By considering public opinion data on free press rights against the backdrop of modern First Amendment jurisprudence, we seek to offer new and original insights into the nature of popular support for these rights – and, in the process, we hope to provide a more sophisticated understanding of how the U.S. democratic system actually works. Our ultimate findings in this respect are as comforting as they are counterintuitive: Specifically, we argue that public support for the constitutional right to a free press remains as strong as ever, even as its most visible practitioners find themselves increasingly under siege.

In offering this argument, we stake a position in that age-old debate over the true value and worth of public opinion. Students and practitioners of politics have long wrestled with the question of whether the masses are capable of conceptualizing (and thus meaningfully contributing to) the democratic process. Such a question is especially important when posed during times of duress, when many citizens' normal conceptions of the world are bombarded by a series of outrageous events. In this book we identify a number of such events that have transfixed the American public in recent years: the O. J. Simpson murder case, the untimely death of Princess Diana of Wales, and the Bill Clinton–Monica Lewinsky affair. Rightly or wrongly, each of these events served as something of a lightning rod for attracting public resentment of the press. Do free press rights become expendable in the public's mind when citizens have grown outraged at the press itself?

Few scholars today would contest the Lockean proposition that the core principle of democracy is to promote and protect the will of the people. Still, questions about the capacity of ordinary citizens to meaningfully contribute to the democratic process are legion. Aristotle and Plato each had serious doubts about the abilities of the masses; James Madison and Alexander Hamilton designed a system of democratic government that protected citizens against the tyranny of the masses; and even in contemporary times, elected officials are criticized for making decisions based on public opinion polls – in fact, many are hailed as "strong" and "bold" leaders simply because they made decisions that run counter to the public mood.

In the 1950s and 1960s, empirical research addressing the capabilities of the masses seemed to confirm the image of a public that lacked informed thought about the political world. Scholars at the University of Michigan wrote off voters and the public as being incapable of rational movements along the liberal–conservative spectrum (Campbell et al., 1960). And Philip Converse's now-classic piece "The Nature of Belief Systems in Mass Publics" (1964) portrays the public as lacking the intellectual fortitude to meaningfully understand and organize political information. Nor did early scholars express much confidence in the masses' capacity to understand and rationally apply essential principles of civil liberties protections. Writing in the period immediately following Senator Joseph McCarthy's rise to power, Samuel Stouffer (1955), for example, concluded that the public was prone to relax principles of civil liberties in favor of its sense of "traditional community" standards. He concluded that public ignorance of both the law and the various nuances of constitutional issues may have clouded its ability to think about civil liberties in a rational manner. Prothro and Grigg (1960) similarly decried the public's inability to think rationally about such constitutional principles. Just as public resentment of the Nazis' march in Skokie, Illinois, reached a fever pitch in 1978, many scholars at that time seemed to take it for granted that the masses would forgo democratic principles of free expression in such controversial circumstances.

For Stouffer, Prothro, and Grigg, consolation could be found only in the willingness of political elites to extend these principles to controversial circumstances. Adamany and Grossman (1983) astutely discovered that certain elites and activists provide enduring support for the Supreme Court during difficult times, as compared with broad-based public support, which on the whole tended to be more hostile. For many scholars, the threat of public outrage thus remained a real, if so far unrealized, one. What if critical elections were to weaken the hold of the Court's ideological allies? Could the public be counted on to withstand the inclination to suppress claimants of controversial rights?

Although the earliest of these empirical studies painted a rather grim portrait of the American public, one notable analyst had come to the ardent defense of the people. In studying voting behavior, V. O. Key Jr. argued in *The Responsible Electorate* (1966) that voters are not fools at all – that they are actually moved by central and relevant questions of public policy. Thus, according to Key, when it came to explaining public ignorance, it was the political environment itself that subverted the ability of the public to act rationally. *The Responsible Electorate* led to a reconsideration of the rationality of the public and its capacity for responsibly contributing to the democratic process. Numerous influential scholars who followed Key aggressively revisited the question of the masses' abilities and arrived at more optimistic conclusions about the public's ability to contribute rationally to democracy. Benjamin Page and Robert Shapiro's *The Rational Public* (1992) represents perhaps the most elegant articulation of Key's premise in recent years. Studying hundreds of opinion surveys conducted between 1935 and 1990, they concluded that the American public in fact holds a number of real, stable, and sensible opinions about public policy and that these opinions develop and change in a reasonable fashion based on changing circumstances and the introduction of new information.

Despite the strides taken in public opinion research in recent years, commentators continue to express considerable doubts about the public's ability to appreciate the importance of free expression rights in the U.S. polity. Perhaps this skepticism arises because Supreme Court opinions, which commonly define the formal limits and boundaries of such constitutional rights, are so difficult for the average citizen to digest. Or perhaps it stems from the nature of these civil liberties conflicts themselves: The right of a controversial (and sometimes quite offensive) minority is usually in conflict with either the majority of the community or a victimized member of that community who may evoke considerable sympathy. Public opinion research is replete with doubts about the public's capacity to see beyond the particular facts of the case to the larger concerns of constitutional rights protections for the minority. In the most comprehensive study to date of public support for the Bill of Rights, McCloskey and Brill (1983) resigned themselves to the fact that large segments of the population were simply unable to internalize such important libertarian norms.

This book extends the rational public theory to the mass public's view of free expression rights generally, and of the freedom of the press in particular. Specifically, we reconsider allegations of "irrationality," "fickleness," and "inconsistency" that so many others have leveled at the masses. Through analysis of two original, large-scale national surveys, conducted in 1997 and 1999, we explore the framework through which the public views and applies the rights of free press in the contemporary media age. To that end, we also assess levels of public knowledge and awareness of these free press rights, and the orientation of the public toward abstract and concrete support for free press rights. Ultimately, we conclude that the mass public applies press freedoms in a logical and consistent manner. In fact, the public is nearly as consistent as the courts – and more consistent than most politicians – in the way it applies crucial First Amendment rights to members of the press. The original paradigm of a public incapable of making the hard decisions necessary to sustain a free democracy is thus turned on its head in this critical context.

We also examine the tension that arises between positive attitudes about the value of press freedoms as a principle of free expression and negative attitudes about the performance of the modern media. In an age when confidence in the press has declined in the eyes of so many citizens, is there a concomitant negative influence on popular perceptions of "free press" principles? To answer that question, we document negative feelings about the contemporary media, as well as attitudes about press freedoms. Here, too, we discover a public that is both capable of and willing to distinguish between a poorly performing media on one hand and the importance of a constitutionally guaranteed freedom of the press in U.S. society on the other hand. These are healthy signs indeed for a democracy that depends on the support of its citizens. And they provide further evidence of a public that is, at least collectively speaking, quite rational.

We are grateful to a number of people who have supported us in writing this book. Many of our colleagues in the Political Science Department at the University of Connecticut provided guidance and support as we prepared the manuscript. We would especially like to thank our chairman, John Rourke, as well as George Cole and Rudy Tokes, each of whom provided us with detailed feedback on the manuscript. Rich Hiskes helped us think through some of the theoretical implications of our work. Michael Cornfield played a crucial role as a sounding board for many of our ideas, both large and small. Our colleague and close friend Sam Best also deserves a special note of thanks for helping us with the final stages of editing. At the Center for Survey Research and Analysis, Chris Barnes, Catherine Salai, Lisa Tortora, Nancy Barth, Chase Harrison, Rich Clark, Jennifer Dineen, Erin St. Onge, Lily Markons, Melanie Chebro, and Lori Kalinowski contributed to the integrity of the surveys that serve as the basis for our findings. Bob Shapiro at Columbia University also made numerous suggestions on the manuscript that greatly improved our work.

We are particularly indebted to the Freedom Forum and the First Amendment Center for commissioning and funding the survey work. The Center's dedication to First Amendment freedoms is unwavering, and the commitment of Larry McGill, Ken Paulson, and Paul McMasters to public opinion research on First Amendment principles provides an invaluable service to our understanding of democracy in America.

It was also a pleasure to work with Lewis Bateman and his colleagues at Cambridge University Press. The quality of such a distinguished institution speaks for itself, and the integrity of the people who worked with our manuscript there was unmatched. The two reviewers also provided important feedback that substantially improved our work. Of course we alone are responsible for whatever errors remain.

We'd also like to thank our families – Andrea, Mary Beth, Rachel, Jane, Kenny, and Allison – for supporting us and not making us feel too guilty for spending many late evenings and weekends hard at work rather than with them while we completed this project.

But most of all, we'd like to thank each other. Embarking on such a large project as the research and preparation of a scholarly book is a daunting task. In all frankness, we did so with little knowledge of each other at the outset, and that was a risk. Several years later, we see it as a risk wisely taken.

January 2001
Storrs, Connecticut

1

Freedom of the Press
and the Power of Public Opinion

The press in the United States has become a modern-day whipping boy for frustrated citizens. Its detractors are many and its supporters are few. According to one recent survey, Americans trust newspaper reporters to tell the truth only slightly more than they trust either politicians or lawyers to do so.[1] Nor does the public think much of journalists' ethical standards, ranking them on a par with those of elected officials, attorneys, and corporate executives.[2] Spurred by the growing chasm that has developed between members of the communications media and the public, legal experts have begun to predict dire consequences for Americans' First Amendment rights (see, e.g., Richards, 1998; Sanford, 1999). One commentator has even argued that the First Amendment as a whole is "more under siege now than ever before in this country's history" (Richards, 1998:1). Such doomsday talk assumes that the public's lack of confidence in the media translates readily into weakened support for freedom of the press.

---

[1] "Americans' Views of the News: What They Like, What They Don't Like, and What Sources They Use." Study Sponsored by the Freedom Forum, conducted by the Roper Center for Public Opinion Research, University of Connecticut, February 1997, p. 12. According to the survey, only 31 percent indicated that they trusted "most" or "all" of what newspaper reporters say, as compared with 31 percent for their own congressperson, 29 percent for the president, and 23 percent for lawyers. By contrast, 77 percent indicated they trusted most or all of what a member of the clergy says, and 70 percent trusted most or all of what a medical doctor says.

[2] Ibid. When asked whether the ethical standards of various professions were either "very high, high, average, low, or very low," 19 percent ranked the standards of newspaper reporters and TV reporters as either "high" or "very high," as compared with 15 percent for elected officials and lawyers and 13 percent for corporate executives. Meanwhile, 75 percent rated the ethical standards of priests, ministers, and rabbis as high or very high, ranking the clergy slightly higher than teachers (68 percent) and medical doctors (60 percent).

1

This book approaches the problem of public dissatisfaction with the media from an entirely different perspective. Specifically, we argue that public sentiment toward press freedoms is *not* as fragile as many scholars suggest. Certainly the relationship between the public and the media promises to remain a complicated one for the foreseeable future. As always, popular support for the press as a whole is a product of the current political environment, as well as various historical, social, and pragmatic considerations. Yet, at least for the time being, a relatively sophisticated public continues to differentiate between members of the press and the critical function they perform in a democracy. In short, the constitutionally guaranteed freedom of the press appears to be weathering the storm of criticisms that has been leveled at those who most often exercise that very freedom.

The distinction we draw throughout this book between public support for the press on one hand and public support for the freedoms exercised by the press on the other is a significant one. It is certainly debatable whether public dissatisfaction with the media alone can inhibit democracy, but popular support for constitutional rights such as freedom of the press is a necessary precondition to the survival of those democratic freedoms. Writing to James Madison prior to the formation of the new American government, Thomas Jefferson argued passionately for a bill of rights: "it is what the people are entitled to against every government on earth, general or particular, and what no government should refuse, or rest on inference."[3] Having seen the Virginia Bill of Rights violated "in every instance where it had been opposed to a popular current," Madison viewed this formal list of liberties with considerably less enthusiasm. He responded to Jefferson: "experience proves the inefficacy of a bill of rights on those occasions when its controul [sic] is most needed. ... Repeated violations of these parchment barriers have been committed by overbearing majorities in every State."[4]

Jefferson's argument eventually carried the day: In 1791 a federal bill of rights proposed by the first Congress was ratified by the necessary three-fourths of the state legislatures. Nevertheless, Madison's initial trepidation[5] proved well founded in the long run, as First Amendment

---

[3] Letter, Thomas Jefferson to James Madison, December 20, 1787 (Papers 12:44), in Philip B. Kurland and Ralph Lerner, eds., *The Founders' Constitution* (Chicago: University of Chicago Press, 1987), p. 457.

[4] Letter, James Madison to Thomas Jefferson, October 17, 1788 (Papers 11:297–300), in Philip B. Kurland and Ralph Lerner, eds., *The Founders' Constitution* (Chicago: University of Chicago Press, 1987), p. 477.

[5] Madison must have overcome the objections he voiced to Jefferson; as a representative from Virginia in the first Congress, Madison became one of the principal sponsors of the proposed Bill of Rights.

rights that might have otherwise appeared secure were still cast aside at critical moments in U.S. history. Unfortunate examples of this phenomenon abound: the jailing of "disloyal" citizens under the late-eighteenth-century Alien and Sedition Acts, the prosecution of critical newspaper editors during the Civil War, the increased reliance by government officials on anti-Communist loyalty oaths during the Red Scare of the 1940s. Just as Madison warned, flagging public support for any provision of the Bill of Rights, including the freedom of the press, may render that provision a mere "parchment barrier" offering little of value to individuals who seek a safe harbor in its written promise.

Throughout this book therefore we evaluate the current state of press freedoms in the United States by analyzing public support *both* for the press itself and for the rights exercised by members of the press. This dichotomy between public approval of a particular freedom and public support for the individuals and groups most commonly associated with the exercise of that freedom is not unique to this context. Certainly some provisions of the Bill of Rights are deemed controversial *precisely because those who rely most on those provisions evoke negative feelings from the public.* Thus, for example, the Fifth Amendment's privilege against self-incrimination – as enforced through an exclusionary rule that forbids the admission of unduly coerced confessions in a court of law – fails to engender enthusiastic public support in part because its principal beneficiaries are thought to be hardened criminals. Nor should we anticipate that the Eighth Amendment's protection against "cruel and unusual punishment" will ever serve as much of a barrier against exceedingly tough law enforcement measures: Legislators rarely enhance their own electoral hopes when they defend rights claimed by convicted felons.

By contrast, the discrepancy between support for rights and the groups that exercise those rights is much more discernible in other contexts. Abstract rights of free assembly generally solicit few objections, even though groups like the Nazis and the Ku Klux Klan are among the most frequent claimants of those rights. And the abstract right to the free exercise of religion has always generated considerable public support, even though Jehovah's Witnesses, the Amish, and more extreme "fringe groups" are the most frequent claimants of such rights. None of the groups just mentioned enjoys widespread public sympathy; they are either groups that evoke considerable hostility (e.g., the Nazis and the KKK) or that remain little known (and perhaps also misunderstood) by the general public. Regardless, the abstract rights those groups so often claim appear to "transcend" the popularity of the groups themselves, making public support for the abstract claim far more sustainable in the long run.

At this point in U.S. history, the status that free press rights enjoy in our democracy is a source of heightened concern, if only because the status and prestige of the press itself now rest on such weak footing. Focusing on events from the past decade that received intensive coverage in the press – including the highly visible Clinton-Lewinsky affair – allows us to first assess public support for this First Amendment guarantee at the turn of the twenty-first century and then compare that level of support with analogous levels of support indicated in previous years. Has the public lost confidence in the press, and if so, why? More important, if such a decline in confidence has occurred, how might that decline affect Americans' views of the constitutional guarantees of the freedom of the press in general? Should we be worried about the long-term implications that such a decline may have on a well-functioning democracy? Two large-scale national studies of American attitudes toward the press conducted in 1997 and 1999 provide the primary sources of data for this systematic examination of the current state of press freedoms.[6]

THE AMERICAN PRESS UNDER FIRE

Numerous facts brought to light in several recent lawsuits against the media have contributed to the "piling on" of criticism against members of the press. Critics of the media have interpreted these cases to be symptomatic of an overall shift in the public's positive understanding of the role played by the press in a democracy. Some scholars (e.g., Sanford, 1999) have even suggested that the recent string of increased jury awards and settlements could represent the final nail in the coffin for free press rights. Consider three especially high-profile lawsuits that plaintiffs have brought against media defendants in recent years:

- In January 1997, a federal court jury in North Carolina awarded to Food Lion, the 1,100-store supermarket chain, a $5.5 million judgment against the American Broadcasting Company (ABC). Food Lion had originally sued ABC after learning that the network had used videos secretly made by reporters who had obtained jobs at two of its supermarkets. The videos showed the stores in question selling spoiled meat and cheese that had been exposed to rats. Yet it was the broadcast reporters – and not Food Lion – who suffered the greater legal liability. Only $1,402 of the judgment represented compensatory damages; the rest amounted to punitive damages assessed by the jury against the network. Eventually a

---

[6] We conducted a brief follow-up survey on public attitudes toward the First Amendment in the spring of 2000; where the findings from that more recent survey add to or modify earlier findings, we provide them for comparative purposes.

federal appeals court threw out all but $2.00 of the damages ordered by the jury. Although reveling in their legal victory, ABC officials knew they had dodged a bullet in the case. After all, a jury of citizens had unequivocally condemned the press's controversial methods. The same legal system might not be so forgiving when presented with similarly aggressive press tactics in the future.

- Paladin Press of Boulder, Colorado, paid an even greater price for its actions. On May 21, 1999, the small independent publisher agreed to stop selling its book *Hit Man: A Technical Manual for Independent Contractors.* The book had billed itself as providing readers with detailed, step-by-step instructions on how to successfully commit murder. James Perry followed the book's suggestions to the letter in the course of murdering two people at the request of Lawrence Horn, an ex-husband of one of the victims. Perry and Horn were prosecuted and held criminally liable for their actions – but the blame did not stop there. The families of the victims also filed suit against Paladin, charging the publisher with aiding and abetting the murders. In addition to ceasing all publication and advertising of the manual, Paladin agreed to a multimillion-dollar settlement of the lawsuit less than a week before a Maryland jury was scheduled to consider the case. Fearful that such a jury might react with outrage, the suddenly cautious publisher cut its losses.

- On February 2, 1999, a federal jury in Portland, Oregon, awarded $107 million in damages to a group of doctors that had sued anti-abortion activists over an Internet site. The controversial World Wide Web site, infamously labeled "The Nuremberg Files," had referred to doctors who perform abortions as "baby butchers" and publicized their names, photos, addresses, and license plate numbers. Although the Web site did not *explicitly* threaten violence against abortion doctors, the jury agreed that its format amounted to a "wanted poster" for such physicians. (Among those listed on the site was Dr. Barnett Slepian, whose name was crossed out within hours of his being killed by a sniper.) The jurors concluded that a "reasonable person" could have considered the harsh words and graphics to be threats. Publishers of the Web site were thus forced to sit in legal limbo for two years, until an appeals court threw the verdict out in March 2001.

Alarmists point to these and other lawsuits as proof that the public's growing distaste for the media has already started to impinge on traditional free press rights. Upon closer inspection, however, each of the cases cited also shows how a failure to properly distinguish hostility to the press from a more general hostility to the *freedom of the press* can lead to unfounded conclusions about the state of our democracy. In the Food Lion case, for example, many viewed the initial jury award as proof that the public had become fed up with aggressive newsgathering tactics – yet the appeals court's subsequent reduction of the award actually brought the trial court more closely in line with the prevailing public opinion of the time. According to a 1997 Media Studies Center/CSRA survey, 55 percent of the public believed that the initial jury award in the case was too severe, nearly double the combined number of respondents who thought it "not severe enough" or "about right." Almost the same percentage (54 percent) said they would have sided with ABC if they had been on a jury, compared with just 16 percent who favored Food Lion.

Similar misunderstandings about the nature of public opinion arose with regard to the other two cases. In the litigation over the *Hit Man* publication, the publisher's fear of going before a jury, where all the gory details of the double murder would be presented, hardly translates into public acceptance of general curtailments on the right to publish freely. To be successful at trial, the plaintiffs would have been forced to show that Paladin acted with "deliberate intent" to encourage or facilitate murder, an extreme factual finding that would have left Paladin a lone pariah even within the publishing industry itself. Despite all the negative media attention given to the "Nuremberg Files" Web site, a clear plurality of the public in 1999 also believed the jury verdict represented a violation of the site authors' First Amendment rights.[7] And indeed, the U.S. Court of Appeals for the Ninth Circuit ultimately vindicated the defendants' First Amendment rights, once again reeling in a jury that had exceeded the limits of the law.

The unique legal posture assumed in these cases may have contributed somewhat to the resulting confusion – each of the three lawsuits represented something of a break from the more classic libel or slander cases that have traditionally dominated the legal landscape. Food Lion charged that ABC reporters had committed fraud, trespass, and breach of loyalty by posing as employees. Paladin was accused of aiding and abetting the commission of murder. And the plaintiffs in the Nuremberg Files case charged the defendants with having issued the equivalent of physical threats; they relished the prospect of a jury eager to parcel out blame for the highly visible murders of abortion doctors.

By contrast, in the more common type of lawsuit filed against the press, a public figure – his or her reputation damaged by false accusations in the press – sues that member of the press or press organization for libel or slander. An entire jurisprudence of press freedoms has evolved

---

[7] This figure comes directly from the CSRA study conducted at the University of Connecticut that is discussed at length in Chapter 2.

around such libel lawsuits. *New York Times v. Sullivan*[8] was the landmark First Amendment case of its generation. In *Sullivan*, Montgomery, Alabama, officials brought a civil libel action against the *New York Times* for the allegedly libelous statements that were made in a full-page advertisement published on March 29, 1960, describing the civil rights movement in the South and concluding with an appeal for funds. The Alabama Supreme Court, seeking to rid the state of a "hostile" newspaper, upheld the lower court's libel judgment of $500,000. Although it was uncontroverted at trial that some of the statements found in the ad were not technically accurate descriptions of the events,[9] the U.S. Supreme Court nevertheless announced a new First Amendment rule to govern all future lawsuits: Public officials would thereafter be prohibited from recovering damages for a defamatory falsehood relating to their official conduct unless they could prove that the statement was made with "actual malice" – in other words, that it was made with knowledge of its falsity or with reckless disregard of whether or not it was false.

In announcing rules that were so highly protective of the freedom of the press, the Supreme Court recognized a "profound national commitment to the principle that debate on public issues should be uninhibited, robust and wide open." For scholars such as Alexander Meiklejohn and Harry Kalven, the *Sullivan* decision was an "occasion for dancing in the streets" (Kalven, 1964). The civil rights movement also celebrated the ruling, as aggressive coverage of news events in the South proved critical to civil rights leaders' hopes of creating a national consensus for reform.

Five years after *Sullivan*, the Warren Court handed down another decision favorable to civil liberties in *Brandenburg v. Ohio*.[10] At a Ku Klux Klan rally held near Cincinnati, Ohio, in the late 1960s, several leaders of the assembled group uttered phrases that were derogatory of Negroes and Jews. One speaker made reference to the possibility that some "revengence" might be taken on government institutions, and another stated his belief that "the nigger should be returned to Africa, the Jew returned to Israel." Charges were brought against the leaders of the rally under the Ohio Criminal Syndicalism Statute, which made it a crime to advocate "the duty, necessity, or propriety of crime, sabotage,

---

[8] 376 U.S. 254 (1964).

[9] The inaccuracies contained within the ad were actually quite trivial. As an example, although African-American students staged a demonstration on the state capitol steps, they sang the national anthem, not "My Country, 'Tis of Thee," as the ad had indicated. And while nine students were expelled by the state Board of Education, the action was not for leading the demonstration at the capitol (as the ad indicated) but for demanding service at a lunch counter in the Montgomery County Courthouse on another day.

[10] 395 U.S. 444 (1969).

violence or unlawful methods of terrorism as a means of accomplishing industrial or political reform." In *Brandenburg*, the Court ruled that free speech rights could only rarely be limited for fear of inciting violence: There must be at once a clear threat of "imminent lawless action," and the words used must be specifically directed to inciting such action. Accordingly, because the Ohio Criminal Syndicalism Statute had punished mere advocacy, it fell within the condemnation of the First Amendment.

Certainly *New York Times v. Sullivan* enjoys reverential status among those who support a broad interpretation of press freedoms under the First Amendment. But at first glance, *Brandenburg*'s significance in this context may be more difficult to see. Although not normally considered a case involving press freedoms, *Brandenburg* – in combination with *Sullivan*'s heightened protection of the media from libel suits – has had profound implications on press organizations and publishers. Newspapers, magazines, and other publications are now free to serve as outlets for the most extreme and offensive arguments made in society, and those willing to provide such forums can do so with little or no fear that their publications will be held liable. Not surprisingly, in the *Hit Man* litigation described previously, *Brandenburg v. Ohio* became the centerpiece of extended discussion among lawyers arguing both sides of the case (Smolla, 1999).

Who benefits from this liberal jurisprudence of free press rights? Theoretically, the legal precedents described here should be of assistance to any and all members of the "press" hoping to escape challenges to their discretion to publish. Included in that group of beneficiaries are not simply members of the so-called "traditional press establishment" – that is, those who are routinely issued "press credentials" or who work for press organizations that are known within the larger community. Perhaps a book on public opinion written three decades ago would have been forced to work within such a restrictive definition of the press, or risk straying far beyond the bounds of what the public perceives of as the "press." Yet in the modern media age of the late twentieth and early twenty-first centuries, that conventional definition of "press" no longer holds much weight with the public. Today the public relies on far more than television, radio, and print journalists to provide it with news and information. The onset of the electronic age in publishing renders most of these older definitions inapplicable. According to one survey,[11] a full quarter of the American public in 1997 routinely relied on the Internet

---

[11] This finding comes from a February 1997 survey commissioned by the Newseum in Arlington, Virginia, and conducted by the Center for Survey Research and Analysis at the University of Connecticut.

or an online service for some of its news; by the fall of 2000, that number had risen to a full 54 percent of the American public. And not all of these Internet news sources are run by so called "established" journalists. By some estimates, Internet columnist Matt Drudge, an at-home computer publisher, enjoyed a far greater audience during the Clinton-Lewinsky scandal than did *Slate*, *Salon*, or any other of the more heavily funded Internet news magazines. Changes in the rules of the media game force a change not only in public perceptions of the press but also in the way social scientists must go about measuring those perceptions.

Given the increased reliance by the public on less conventional news sources, the definition of the term "freedom of the press" must expand accordingly. Rather than rely on outdated and unworkable distinctions between the "mainstream" and "nonmainstream" press outlets, we use a more all-encompassing definition of freedom of the press. For purposes of this work, any organization or person who gives publicity to sentiments, opinions, or other information through a medium (including electronic media) may stake a rightful claim to those freedoms provided to members of the press. In theory, such a definition encompasses not only "major" media organizations such as ABC but also lesser-known publishers such as Paladin Press and Internet publishers such as those that produced "The Nuremburg Files." With the popularization of the Internet, press freedoms are now applicable to any individual with a desktop computer and a modem.

Monetary verdicts against media organizations for libel soared in the 1990s. Yet as we have already noted, none of the three cases highlighted earlier in this chapter featured typical libel or slander claims. Instead, lawyers faced with the task of constructing legal challenges to press organizations have been working overtime in recent years, crafting innovative lawsuits designed to circumvent the high barrier offered by the First Amendment's freedom of the press. This litigation trend attests to the relative strength of press freedoms in the United States, rather than to their gradual demise. Those who would read too much into the rare extravagant verdicts that are upheld on appeal may be doing a disservice to the discussion as well: Before any such verdict can be rendered, a judge must first determine that there exists at least an arguable, factual basis for the allegations being made against that media defendant. Thus, *the fact that press organizations may be more frequently abusing their freedom does* not *necessarily mean that the freedom itself has diminished*. In fact, the opposite might just as well be true: Given finite resources, a string of negative jury verdicts may cause judges to constrict (rather than broaden) the pool of allowable complaints against the press, lest their courtrooms be overrun with far more complaints than they can handle. In this book we choose to look beyond such crude indicators to gauge the real effect Americans' distaste for the media has had on support for press freedoms.

Members of the press likely do not welcome the proliferation of innovative lawsuits being brought against them. Such lawsuits tap into a clear sentiment of hostility the American public has increasingly felt toward the press. The Supreme Court handed down its decisions in *Sullivan* and *Brandenburg* during the 1960s, a period in U.S. history when newspapers and other media organizations were often celebrated as heroes. Consider the *Sullivan* case, which epitomized the war over civil rights being waged around the country. Like many other news organizations, the *New York Times*, reporting to a national audience about resistance to civil rights initiatives in the South, feared retribution from hostile southern juries in the form of disproportionate libel judgments. Prior to the *Sullivan* decision itself – which reversed a half-million-dollar judgment against the newspaper – such fears were hardly unfounded.

During the 1970s, CBS anchor Walter Cronkite became a national icon; in one survey conducted during that period, 73 percent of the public judged him to be "the most trusted figure in American public life."[12] Cronkite's nightly broadcasts were a cultural fixture, symbolic of the positive connection that existed between the public at large and the press. Then, when corruption pervaded the highest levels of the federal government during the 1970s, it was the press that garnered the bulk of the credit in the public's eyes. The Vietnam War was the first military conflict to feature television reporters on the battlefield. Network correspondents and investigative print reporters such as Sydney Schanberg of the *New York Times* filed daily reports that exposed patterns of deception by high-level officials and laid bare "the bright shining lie" perpetuated by the government. Not surprisingly, the public rushed to credit the *Washington Post* with helping to bring about the demise of Richard Nixon's presidency in 1974. Never mind that John Dean, Alexander Butterfield, Sam Ervin, Howard Baker, Archibald Cox, and Leon Jaworski, among others, were also key contributors to Nixon's downfall during the Watergate affair. Each of those individuals was identified with the government; none enjoyed the same cherished place in the American psyche that reporters did during that same era. There was far more intrinsic appeal to the story of two little-known *Washington Post* reporters, Bob Woodward and Carl Bernstein, who persisted against overwhelming odds to uncover the facts of White House corruption. These events nurtured a positive relationship between the press and the public.

---

[12] The Gallup poll, conducted in 1973, ranked Cronkite 15 points higher than President Nixon. See Richard Snow, "He Was There." *American Heritage*, December 1, 1994, p. 42.

Contrast those relatively positive public images of the press from several decades ago with the negative images of the press that predominate today. Whereas the press previously enjoyed the benefit of the doubt from large majorities of the public, Americans today have grown far more cynical about the benefits of an aggressive press. Some factors contributing to this rise in distrust are of course structural in nature. The proliferation of cable channels and Internet news sources has diluted the overall quality of news. Now anyone who can rent a local cable access channel or maintain a personal Web page can become a publisher of news and information of interest to the public and can make that information accessible immediately. These changes in the nature and variety of news organizations and publishing units have transformed the relationship between the people and the press.

Additionally, larger press organizations must fight for their piece of an ever-shrinking pie of revenue from consumers who enjoy numerous low-cost or even free news alternatives. As a consequence, news organizations in recent years have increasingly tailored their agendas toward grabbing the immediate interest of the public, rather than toward more comprehensive reporting on issues of national importance (Davis and Owen, 1998). Additionally, the public no longer feels that a robust press is as necessary to uncover important facts, as many different types and varieties of information are now freely available on the Internet for the public's own perusal and original interpretation.

Moreover, Americans may not trust the press to the same degree as before because increased competition among a larger number of news sources means greater exposure of each news organization's failures. Certainly the public may view some news sources ("The Jerry Springer Show," the *National Enquirer*, etc.) as so irresponsible or sensationalistic that their errors or misinformation cannot be held to any reasonable standards of journalistic integrity. But in the case of well-respected press organizations, every mistake or error is sure to garner the attention of the competition, and a considerable amount of negative coverage as well. For example, NBC's failure to clearly label a car crash as an artificial simulation on its program "Dateline" attracted negative coverage for months. CBS's decision to electronically superimpose its own logo over an NBC billboard at Times Square during New Year's Eve 1999 also attracted negative attention. Taken together, these incidents and others encourage the public to be even more wary of the press.

More often than not, the press has also been its own worst enemy in failing to maintain a relationship of respect and trust with the public. Three "media events" of the past decade in particular have gone a long way toward reinforcing negative perceptions of the press in the public's mind.

The O. J. Simpson Case and Its Aftermath

Beginning with the infamous police chase of his white Bronco truck on June 17, 1994, the public's interest in O. J. Simpson would become a fixture of media coverage for approximately two and a half years. It was a story that included all the ingredients of a captivating novel: the handsome, former Heisman Trophy–winning, all-pro running back; his glamorous ex-wife; an interracial marriage; a posh southern California estate; and the ill-fated attempt by Simpson to escape the police, as played out on the California highways, live on national television. All these elements combined to ignite the public's interest from the outset. No matter how the media had chosen to cover the events surrounding Simpson's subsequent trial, its members would have no doubt suffered in the eyes of an increasingly cynical public. But the press did little to help its own cause. Hour-by-hour coverage and updates of the Simpson murder case only reinforced the perception (whether accurate or not) that the press was somehow trying to capitalize on this human tragedy to increase the size of its audience. Judge Lance Ito's weak control of the trial (televised around the clock on CNN and Court TV) allowed lawyers to "play to the cameras" and become recognizable media stars in their own right. Little changed after Simpson's acquittal on murder charges in the fall of 1995; coverage of the Brown and Goldman families' civil lawsuit against Simpson, as well as the battle over custody of Simpson's two children, received intense press coverage. On the day the civil trial verdicts were handed down, two of the three networks actually broke into live coverage of President Clinton's State of the Union address to report the outcomes. For better or worse, the public's lasting image of the O. J. Simpson case was not simply of a heinous murder that went unpunished; it was also of a horde of exploitative broadcast and print reporters gathered outside a Los Angeles County courthouse, day after day.

Princess Diana's Death

Unlike in the O. J. Simpson case, press organizations rushing to cover the death of Princess Diana of Wales in September 1997 had to overcome a deficit in positive perceptions from the outset. Because the aggressiveness of the European "paparazzi" played some arguable role in the car accident that led to her death, Europeans and Americans alike were suspicious of what role the press might play in covering the events after her death. Diana's death also occurred just as several new news sources were being introduced to American audiences, including a second all-news network, MSNBC (co-sponsored by NBC and Microsoft). Coverage of Diana's death, her funeral, and the roles played by other members of the Royal family in its aftermath captured the media's around-the-clock attention. Of course the Royal family has long received saturation coverage from the worldwide press. But the press still failed to distinguish itself in this instance, focusing on petty squabbles: first, between the Queen and Prince Charles, and then later, between Diana's brother and the entire Royal family. That the public "lapped up" these stories is beyond dispute; but by catering to such interests, the press failed to enhance public perceptions of the job it was doing overall.

The Clinton-Lewinsky Story

President Clinton's sexual liaison with Monica Lewinsky, a White House intern, and his subsequent attempts to hide the affair combined to become the single most heavily covered event of the decade, if not of the past several decades. Part of what spurred on the story's relentless press coverage were the graphic sexual details that became public early on. Most press organizations began their coverage of the affair amid a nebulous cloud of rumors in January 1998. Slowly, as more and more facts of the affair became known, the press was able to fill out the contours of the story for an interested public. Public support for the press was already ebbing when the story began, a product of negative feelings cultivated during the past decade by a number of events, including coverage of the O. J. Simpson and Princess Diana stories. But instead of allaying public qualms about an irresponsible press, news organizations only gave credence to those doubts. MSNBC adopted the Lewinsky story as its own and was soon dubbed the network that brought us "all Monica, all the time." Independent publishers on the Internet reveled in the challenge of out-scooping mainstream news organizations; Matt Drudge and other reporters became instant celebrities despite their occasional failure to verify the stories they published. And whenever a news organization got the story wrong – as it appeared when the *Dallas Morning News* retracted a story reporting the existence of a cocktail dress with the president's semen on it – the public crucified the press for jumping the gun in its feverish attempt to "get the president" or "sell newspapers." Never mind that in the long run, the story turned out in fact to be correct; in the minds of the public, the coverage of the Clinton-Lewinsky affair was not the press's finest hour.

So far we have reviewed mostly anecdotal and qualitative evidence of this decline in public support for the press. In the section that follows, we examine a number of recent studies of public opinion to quantitatively assess how public support for the press has dissipated during the past two decades. Specifically, how much has the press declined in the public's eyes? And what role have recent events played in this decline?

MEASURING THE DECLINE IN POPULAR SUPPORT
FOR THE PRESS

Public assessments of the performance of the news media have been on a long-term decline in the United States (Dautrich and Hartley, 1999). This consistent downward trend in evaluations of the press may be indicative of a dysfunction in the American political system as a whole. As we noted previously, members of the press serve a critically important function in our democratic system. Low levels of support, trust, and confidence in the press may be a sign that the masses lack broad positive feelings for this political institution. Without this broad confidence in and affection for the press, citizens may use the press less, and when they do use it, they might be skeptical of its products, such as information used to make voting decisions. At first glance, it may seem that a popular press is a necessary precondition to public affinity for its service to democracy. Yet as it turns out, the important roles the press plays in informing, signaling, and educating the American public may or may not become debilitated by such growing levels of dissatisfaction.

To be sure, public confidence in the press has dropped precipitously over the past several decades. The Gallup Organization has been tracking the level of confidence that Americans have in the news media for many years. Between 1979 and 1999, the Gallup poll found that those expressing either a "great deal" or "quite a lot" of confidence in newspapers dropped from 51 percent to 33 percent. Also, Gallup began tracking confidence in television news in 1993, when 46 percent of the public had either "a great deal" or "quite a lot" of confidence. In 1999, only 34 percent expressed at least "quite a lot" of confidence in television news.

Other surveys indicate the same downward trend. The Yankelovich Group measured public confidence in journalism at 50 percent in 1988. By 1993, confidence in journalism had waned to 25 percent. Similarly, the National Opinion Research Center's trend data show that in the 1970s the press enjoyed higher levels of confidence than political institutions such as Congress and the presidency. By the 1980s, NORC's measure of public confidence in the press had dipped to the 15–20 percent range. And by the 1990s, just 10 percent of the public expressed a high level of confidence in the press.

There is some evidence that the decline in confidence in and opinions about the press may be contributing to a decline in public use of the press. A Pew Center survey conducted during the 1996 presidential election campaign, for example, points to a significant decline in the use of television to get election news (Pew Report, April 1996). In addition, others (Matlin, 1997) have demonstrated a decline in newspaper readership over the past several decades. Among the various reasons cited for the decline in American confidence in the press are: (1) public distaste for particular newsgathering practices (Dautrich and Hartley, 1999; Schudson, 1995; Patterson, 1993); (2) sensationalistic reporting; (3) excessive focus on particular stories; (4) the negative orientation of news (Ansolabehere and Iyengar, 1995; Taylor, 1990; Robinson and Sheehan, 1983; Sabato, 1993); (5) an inappropriate focus on the personal lives of public people; (6) the propensity to highlight conflict (Jamieson, 1992; Bennett, 1980; Anderson and Thorson, 1989); (7) fragmentation of stories in the form of sound bites (Hallin, 1990; Bennett, 1980); (8) inaccuracy of news reporting (Epstein, 1975); (9) inappropriate and excessive press commentary on stories; and (10) political bias in reporting (Hofstetter, 1976; Dautrich and Hartley, 1999; Weaver, 1972; Stevenson and Greene, 1980).

Yet ultimately it is specific events covered by the press that create lasting impressions in the public's mind and thus contribute most to the long-term decline in support described here. Which events have made the most lasting impressions in this regard? Public opinion studies of news coverage of particular events such as presidential elections, U.S. military actions, or terrorist acts (among other things) have shown the public to be increasingly critical of the press's coverage of those events. Of course the news event of modern times that – because of its salience, level of coverage, and longevity in the news – epitomized public dissatisfaction with contemporary coverage of news was the Clinton-Lewinsky story. A series of five surveys conducted by CSRA at the University of Connecticut from January 1998 through March 1999 on public attitudes about coverage of the Clinton-Lewinsky story provides a fairly representative sense of modern public disappointments with the press.

In addition to being a broad-based, highly reported story, the Clinton-Lewinsky affair also featured many of the same elements that have led scholars, pundits, and media analysts to sharply criticize contemporary news reporting. In fact, the scope and exhaustiveness of the press's presentation of the Clinton-Lewinsky story became fodder for critics to use in pointing out the failures of the news to the American public. It is useful, then, to review some of the specific complaints about press coverage of the Clinton-Lewinsky story as a way to understand broader dissatisfaction the public has with press coverage in America.

The American public was highly critical of the "overcoverage" of the Clinton-Lewinsky story. The CSRA survey conducted several weeks after the story broke found that fully 80 percent of the public said that coverage of the story was "excessive." One year later, in a March 1999 survey, fully 87 percent said that the word "excessive" described coverage of the story. Further, two-thirds of the public in February 1998

Table 1.1. Public Interest in Clinton-Lewinsky Story Compared with
other Stories

"I am going to read a list of topics. Please tell me how interested you are in news
about each."

	Very Interested	Somewhat Interested	Not very Interested	Not Interested
Clinton-Lewinsky	4%	14%	23%	59%
Y2K	34	38	13	15
Kosovo/Yugoslavia	19	43	16	14
Social Security	68	27	2	2

Note: Table excludes those saying "don't know."
Source: CSRA University of Connecticut Survey, March 1999.

disagreed that the "Clinton-Lewinsky story is important enough to
deserve the level of coverage that it has received," and six in ten continued to disagree with this in October 1998. By March 1999, fully 71
percent disagreed with this statement, with as many as 54 percent
"strongly" disagreeing. Clearly, most members of the public believed the
story did not deserve the level and magnitude of coverage it had received.

Supporting these findings, the surveys also showed that most Americans felt that coverage of the story was characterized by excessive details.
Our survey asked in March 1999: "Imagine that you had been in charge
of news coverage of the Clinton-Lewinsky story. If you had been in
charge, would you have presented more details about the story, fewer
details, or about the same amount?" Sixty percent of respondents said
that they would have presented fewer details had they been in charge.
As seen in Table 1.1, the public's perceived "overkill" of the Clinton-
Lewinsky story was further substantiated by a March 1999 survey
finding that levels of interest in the story were relatively low compared
with those of other stories in the news. Only about one in twenty Americans said they were "very" interested in the Clinton-Lewinsky story, and
less than 20 percent were at least somewhat interested in it. This compares to the vast majority of Americans who expressed at least some
interest in stories about the "Y2K problem," the Kosovo situation, and
discussion of reforming the Social Security system.

Americans also expressed a fair amount of skepticism about the
accuracy of reporting on the Clinton-Lewinsky story. Frequent stories
that used unnamed sources may have contributed to this cynicism. For
example, 64 percent said the media were not taking care to make sure

that the facts were checked before reporting on this story, and about six in ten disagreed with the statement "The news media are reporting the story based on information from reliable sources."

Related to the issue of perceived accuracy in the news is the issue of both the reliability of news sources and the propriety of using anonymous sources in news stories. In October 1998, we asked our sample of Americans the following question: "Since grand jury testimony is supposed to be kept secret, much of the news coverage of the Clinton-Lewinsky story has been based on information leaked to the media by anonymous sources. Do you agree or disagree that using anonymous sources was an appropriate way for the media to report on this?" Fully 70 percent of the public disagreed with the use of anonymous sources in covering the story, with as much as 54 percent "strongly" disagreeing.

Our set of surveys on attitudes about coverage of the story also indicates public concern regarding the motivations of the news media in providing the high level of coverage that they did. The data indicate that the vast majority of Americans perceived that the motivations to cover the story were based more on the desire for ratings than on investigating the facts and reporting the news. For example, in a survey conducted in February 1998, 81 percent said that the news media were focusing heavily on this story "more because they were interested in attracting a large audience" rather than because they were "interested in getting to the bottom of the story." Only 14 percent said they thought the news media were heavily focusing coverage on Clinton-Lewinsky because they wanted to get to the bottom of the story.

Many scholars and analysts criticize the performance of the news media because they claim that the news tends to be of a sensational nature. This includes, among other things, focusing on sexual behavior and content. The focus on the sexual aspects of this story characterized much of the coverage. In a March 1999 CSRA survey, respondents were asked: "Imagine that you were in charge of news coverage of the Clinton-Lewinsky story. If you were in charge would you have included fewer references to sex, more references to sex, or about the same amount of references to sex in news coverage?" Fully 73 percent said they would have included fewer references to sex in their coverage. Americans clearly felt that the sexual material about the story presented to them was excessive. This is, perhaps, what led majorities of Americans to agree that the terms "disgusting" (71 percent) and "embarrassing" (57 percent) appropriately described the news media's coverage of the Clinton-Lewinsky story.

Critics of the modern media point out that the press today is much more willing (and anxious) to focus on the private lives of public people.

The blurring of the line between what is public and what is private and the extent to which private matters represent suitable material for the press remain hotly debated. Certainly, this debate was waged in the context of the Clinton-Lewinsky story. From the public's viewpoint, the press crossed the line and went too far in probing Clinton's personal affairs. When asked what they felt about the media's job in disclosing the details of President Clinton's personal life, 60 percent in February 1998 said the press had gone too far in discussing the president's personal life, 28 percent said they thought the media went about as far as was right, and 9 percent said they had not gone far enough. One year later, in March 1999, 68 percent of Americans felt the press had gone too far in talking about Clinton's personal life, 24 percent said they had gone about as far as was right, and 7 percent said they had not gone far enough.

A final area of media criticism we explore here is the level of commentary journalists provided on this story. The Sunday talk shows, newspapers, political talk radio, and twenty-four-hour television news shows were filled not only with news reports of events and circumstances related to the Clinton-Lewinsky story but also considerable analysis and commentary on those events. Many critics of the contemporary news media argue that commentary is excessive, and often the line is blurred between what is news and what is commentary. The February 1998 CSRA survey found that almost two-thirds (63 percent) of the public felt that journalists were doing "too much" speculating about what might happen next in reporting on the Clinton-Lewinsky story. Five months later, in July 1998, 58 percent of respondents expressed the same opinion. The public agreed that commentary provided by journalists in covering this story was excessive.

The public's attitudes toward coverage of the Clinton-Lewinsky story, then, appear quite negative. Many of the broader criticisms of media performance seem to apply to coverage of this story, and the public tends to agree with the media's harshest critics. The public largely felt that there was excessive coverage of this story and that it was not important enough to warrant the level of coverage it received. Americans also agreed with the criticism that inaccuracy plagued coverage of the story. This perception was fueled by the widespread use of anonymous sources used in reporting. The public also felt that the news media sensationalized the story by dwelling on the sexual aspects of what occurred as well as that the news crossed the line in terms of focusing too much on the president's personal life and private concerns. Moreover, the public had serious questions about the motivations of the press in providing so much coverage of this story, feeling that coverage was largely influenced by the desire to sell papers and magazines and increase audiences rather than to get to the facts of the events that occurred. And while majorities of Americans perceived coverage to be at least somewhat fair to the key personalities involved, large numbers felt that coverage was unfair, particularly to Clinton.

The findings presented here paint a very grim picture indeed of public evaluations of Clinton-Lewinsky news coverage. The public felt as though such coverage was excessive, crossed the line between the president's private concerns and his public role, engaged too much in commentary, and at times was inaccurate, sensationalistic, and more motivated by ratings than by getting to and reporting the facts. These negative impressions have become more or less characteristic of public evaluations of news coverage more generally.

Clearly the Clinton-Lewinsky affair – like the O. J. Simpson and Princess Diana stories that preceded it – contributed to and affirmed negative perceptions of the press in general. But what's really at stake? If the press suffers blows to its prestige in the public's mind but still goes about reporting the news in a seemingly unfettered fashion, is there really any threat to First Amendment rights? Is popular support for the media a necessary precondition for the legal guarantee of freedom that a free press requires to thrive in a democracy? How long can legal institutions go on protecting press rights when the public remains a constant source of opposition to the press?

THE ROLE OF THE FREE PRESS IN A DEMOCRACY

What explains the deep commitment Americans hold to the principle of a free press? Although freedom of the press enjoys some historical roots in the founding era, the reach of that freedom was originally quite limited. In truth, the generation that adopted the First Amendment based its understanding of the importance of a free press on the writings of that great scribe of English law William Blackstone, who believed that the liberty of the press consisted only of laying "no previous restraints upon publications" (i.e., censorship) – by contrast, "if he publishes what is improper, mischievous, or illegal," that remained a crime that could be punished (Blackstone, 1765). Thus while it stood adamantly opposed to any prior restraints on the press, this early generation of Americans included some who accepted the right of government to punish criticism of official conduct *subsequent* to publication. Notably, while most states adopted their own constitutions with provisions protecting "freedom of the press," they simultaneously adopted statutes punishing seditious libel critical of government officials.

What then was the basis for the passage of the freedom of the press provision found in the First Amendment, which was formally ratified in 1791? The historical backdrop just described suggests an analogous interpretation of the federal constitutional provision, rendering the First Amendment powerless to protect the press against subsequent prosecution. If in fact that was the case, the landscape of press freedoms was altered dramatically in the decade following the First Amendment's passage. Throughout the 1790s most newspapers were party organs dominated by partisans engaging in heated rhetoric that commonly ridiculed public officials (Levy, 1985). In a general attempt to quiet subversion and dissent, President John Adams and the Federalist Party–dominated Congress passed the Alien and Sedition Acts in 1798, which made it a crime punishable by fine or imprisonment to speak disparagingly of the national government or to "hold them up to public ridicule" and thus erode their authority. But while seditious libel prosecutions under the act were consistent with the Blackstonian conception of the free press, such attempts to punish speech fared poorly in the arena of public opinion. Public revulsion with the acts, fueled in large part by the Jeffersonian press, was soon followed by the election in 1800 of Thomas Jefferson as president (along with a Republican Congress), who successfully pushed for their repeal. Thus as Justice William Brennan would argue in the 1960s, although the Supreme Court never directly considered the constitutionality of the Alien and Sedition Acts, "the attack upon [their] validity has carried the day in the court of history."[13] And a legacy of support for a robust press under the First Amendment was born, if a bit belatedly.

To date, prior restraints have only rarely been attempted by government officials. Meanwhile, the Supreme Court has never in its history upheld the prior restraint of a publication against First Amendment challenge, and thus the prohibition of prior restraints creates a truly daunting obstacle for any government officials who may harbor thoughts to the contrary. Nevertheless, Congress's repeal of the Alien and Sedition Acts in 1801 did *not* end all debate over seditious libel in subsequent years, and it certainly did not bring an end to libel suits filed against the press in state and federal courts. Moreover, despite enjoying a special and separate mention in the First Amendment itself, as a matter of law the press has enjoyed no greater privilege than any other member of the public in conducting all aspects of its business, including covering trials, investigating matters of public concern, or protecting the identity of witnesses.

As press organizations continue to find themselves legally accountable for a variety of activities, constitutional theorists have feverishly debated the role of the free press in a democracy. Scholars point to at least four

---

[13] *New York Times v. Sullivan*, 376 U.S. at 276.

theoretical justifications for affording expanded rights to the press in this context.

"Educator of the People"

According to Constitutional scholar Leonard Levy, the pressures engendered by the Sedition Act drove Jeffersonians to originate "so broad a theory of freedom of expression" that they advocated the exemption of political opinions from all legal restraints (Levy, 1985). Broadly understood, those principles of Jeffersonian democracy reject almost all limitations on press organizations under the theory that a democratic society requires the free flow of information. In this context, the news media are depicted as "educator of the masses," gathering and disseminating information about matters of public concern. Such a view of the Fourth Estate is consistent with the premise that the freedom of the press is a right that belongs primarily to citizens at large – by facilitating the free flow of information generally, the press furthers the ability of citizens to exercise other rights as well.

"Watchdog of Government"

The press has been nicknamed the "Fourth Estate," providing the functional equivalent of a separate branch of government charged with "checking" public institutions (Meiklejohn, 1948). Because the press serves a unique quasi-structural role in our constitutional system, some commentators believe it may be deserving of special rights and privileges that would allow it to serve that "watchdog function" most effectively. According to this logic, restrictions on reporters' access to prisons and other public institutions ordinarily closed to the public are inherently illegitimate; nor should courtrooms ever be closed to the press. In acting as government watchdog, the press facilitates self-government, rooting out corruption or other improper government activities deemed not in the public interest.

"Facilitator of Public Debate"

Press organizations may also play a far more subtle role in a democracy. Specifically, newspapers, magazines, and other news sources facilitate the public dialogue and debate over important issues that many deem essential to a healthy democratic system. Op-ed pages and letters to the editor sections provide even underfunded, out-of-the-mainstream speakers with the means to present their arguments to the masses. Many magazines are tailored to present one point of view or the other, feeding debates between warring sides through their respective publications. Even articles written in supposedly nonpartisan, mainstream newspapers such as the *New York Times* and *USA Today* usually endeavor to quote the views of speakers from various sides of issues. In aiding in the ventilation of a variety of viewpoints, the press helps to prevent the entrenchment of prevailing views that might otherwise go unchallenged. And thus by this argument, the press plays a crucial role in helping to realize Justice Oliver Wendell Holmes's metaphor of a "marketplace of ideas."[14]

"An Agency with Special Expertise"

Perhaps the most questionable justification for granting the press broader newsgathering freedoms rests on society's need for a thriving nongovernmental institution with expertise in public matters. Under this theory, broader freedom for the press is warranted because the press is itself a specialized agency with expertise in ferreting out important information, making it available, and then interpreting it for large numbers of people. Many press organizations are governed by internal norms of fairness, reasonable attempts at accuracy, and efforts at impartiality; consequently, the immunity of the press from government regulations may be more appropriate than immunity for other institutions. Of course, any theory that distinguishes members of the press from ordinary citizens on this basis is susceptible to criticism. In particular, some scholars have argued that the elevation of the press to a higher status might cause it to lose touch with the public, in effect diminishing public involvement in the process of political communication (e.g., Leonard, 1986). Still, few would argue with the proposition that reporters and others in the press often know more about these subjects than the average citizen does, if only because they can draw on their own experience covering an issue, take note of its many nuances, and nurture ties to newsmakers with further insights on the subject. Whether or not that "expertise" or "familiarity" justifies special privileges from the Constitution or the public, it speaks volumes for the positive role that the press can play in the political dialogue.

ORGANIZATION OF THIS BOOK

What impact has the public's reaction to recent developments in media coverage had on the functioning of the U.S. democratic system? The nature of public support for freedom of the press in the United States, and the effect that reduced levels of support may have on the internal workings of a democracy, will be explored in the chapters that follow. In this chapter we described the nature of the problem of declining support for the press itself. Anecdotal and empirical evidence points to

---

[14] *Abrams v. United States*, 250 U.S. 616, 630 (1919) (Holmes, J., dissenting).

a severed relationship between the press and the public on a number of fronts. Yet what impact does this breakdown in public support for the media have on a well-functioning democracy? What is truly at stake for the U.S. constitutional system?

In Chapter 2 we discuss how our research makes a contribution to contemporary studies demonstrating how the masses apply a rational approach to their own political orientations. Our findings are consistent with this revisionist approach to understanding the capabilities of masses in a democracy. We also utilize David Easton's "Systems Theory" as an initial framework for addressing the problem of declining support for the press. If the public is truly "rational," as recent scholars have suggested, it may be able to maintain a "reservoir of good will" toward the constitutional freedoms that lie at the foundation of the U.S. political system, even as individual actors are busy abusing that same freedom. We then discuss the various core hypotheses that frame our research concerning public opinion and the freedom of the press. Finally, we lay out the research design and methodology of the findings presented in the chapters that follow.

Chapter 3 explores public knowledge of and appreciation for the freedom of the press generally, and the constitutional rules that govern the press more specifically. The U.S. political system is more susceptible to internal divisions and unrest if public support for important freedoms rests on a thin layer of constitutional understanding. Without both public appreciation and recognition of First Amendment rules, support for those principles may prove fleeting, especially when they carry the greatest importance to the citizenry. After describing and analyzing relevant data on public knowledge and appreciation of press freedoms, we apply our findings to the model of a "rational public" previously discussed. What do the data imply about the reservoir of good will that the public maintains toward the press?

In Chapter 4 we address the traditional gap between abstract attitudes for constitutional freedoms on one hand, and attitudes about concrete applications of those freedoms on the other. Americans appear to hold seemingly contradictory views when they are asked for their reactions to these types of questions in other contexts. Both the broad and the concrete opinions about free press rights are important dimensions of support for freedom of the press in America. For example, Americans tend to overwhelmingly endorse the right of free speech or expression but then shy away from granting protection to controversial speakers such as the Ku Klux Klan. Is there a similar divide in public opinion for abstract and concrete press freedoms? If so, is the public assuming two or more logically contradictory positions, or does the public adopt a more sophisticated approach to the freedom of the press, stopping short of unqualified endorsement for that freedom in the first place? We analyze public opinion data from each of these various perspectives to understand diffuse support for freedom of the press.

Cross-media analysis is the focus of Chapter 5. Specifically, how do public perceptions of the freedoms enjoyed by different types of media (print, broadcast, electronic, etc.) vary, and what are the implications of those variations in support? Are media that can feature more graphic displays of violence or sex, such as television, more susceptible to publicly supported government restrictions than newspapers, magazines, or books? And how does such variance in public opinion square with prevailing judicial precedents on the subject? Does the public favor chilling freedom for some forms of media in particular? More important, we address the question of whether or not the public applies a rational approach in its thinking about how press freedoms ought to be applied. After assessing the implications of different cross-media treatments, we return to the larger issue of democracy. If support for freedom of the press varies based on the type of press organization it flows to, what implications may that development have on future tolerance in the U.S. democratic system, especially in light of the proliferation and expansion of revolutionary new forms of electronic media?

Building off the findings in the previous chapter, Chapter 6 addresses the issue of public opinion for varying sources within a particular medium and again searches for rationality in public thinking regarding the application of press rights. Should different press organizations receive different privileges based on the "quality" of their contributions to the political dialogue? Certainly the public treats information that emanates from mainstream news organizations (the *New York Times*, ABC, etc.) differently from information it receives from little-known news sources or press entities with poor reputations for accuracy ("The Jerry Springer Show," the *National Enquirer*, etc.). When information is processed, the perceived credibility and reputation for accuracy of the news organization plays a critical if not dominant role. Yet do these credibility judgments influence the freedom afforded to different news organizations, all other things being equal? Does the public grant Jerry Springer the same level of freedom that it gives to Peter Jennings and Tom Brokaw? Should all newspapers be treated the same? We compare and contrast the Supreme Court's cautious approach to this subject with public opinion findings on the applicability of press freedoms to different organizations. In the process, even more light is shed on the nature of this reservoir of good will for press freedoms: Is it truly equal freedom for all?

Finally, in Chapter 7 we summarize the findings of this book and discuss their implications for the future of press freedoms in the United

States. Clearly the relationship between the press and the public deteriorated in the 1980s and 1990s; but the press can still draw on the reservoir of good will it enjoys among members of the public. Thus, as our analysis suggests, all hope is not lost. The freedom of the press remains an important value embedded in the American psyche, and what recent media performance has taken away, future performance might just as quickly return.

2

Surveying the Public on Press Freedoms

In Chapter 1 we suggested that – given the right circumstances – the deteriorating reputation of the press as a whole might well place its legitimacy as an American political institution at significant risk. But slipping public support for the press would be especially problematic for the system as a whole if it were to cause equally precipitous drops in public support for the *value* of freedom of the press in America. The U.S. democratic system relies heavily on the free flow of political information and ideas, and this free flow takes place largely through the robust exercise of First Amendment rights by members of the press.

In this chapter, we offer a multi-layered, theoretical framework to guide our investigation of public support for freedom of the press at the turn of the century. To a degree, the systems theory model developed by David Easton (1975) aids our understanding of the relationship among public opinion, the press, and freedom of the press. It is not our intention here to resurrect systems theory, which has suffered its share of criticisms in recent years. Rather, the systems model merely provides a useful framework for structuring our discussion of the relationship between attitudes about the media and attitudes about press freedoms. We use Easton's model merely as a starting point from which we articulate our central thesis and develop specific hypotheses that will be addressed throughout this book.

The second layer of our theoretical framework concerns itself with the way that the "rational public" asserts its interests in a democratic system. Thus, rather than focus simply on the "system" itself, we stake a position in the much larger scholarly debate over the capacity of the masses to participate in democratic rule. Traditionally, many scholars and commentators have questioned the sensibilities of the public in this and other contexts. The research presented in this work speaks forcefully to the opposite position in this great debate.

Finally, we present our research design for studying public support for freedom of the press. This section includes a review of our survey research work, including a presentation of the sampling methodology, a discussion and rationale for the survey instrument content, and a review of the data collection experience. We also describe the key independent variables constructed from the data set on which we rely for our analysis throughout this book.

SYSTEMS THEORY AND PUBLIC SUPPORT OF PRESS FREEDOMS

We have already demonstrated that public opinion in the United States toward the press has deteriorated in recent decades. Yet the more pressing concern of this book is with the extent to which increasingly negative opinions about the press actually affect attitudes about the core liberty of freedom of the press. If the negative view of the press's performance has caused a decline in this core value, then the American political system has suffered a severe blow indeed. A free press and its healthy functioning (as a watchdog, information provider, etc.) are critical to the very legitimacy of the political system.

Certainly it is possible that press freedoms will diminish absent a strong public orientation toward the media. In theory, any reduction in good will toward individual members of the press or particular press institutions could bode poorly for the status of the free press in general; it may have a chilling effect on the news media, its function in the political system, and on the functioning of the democratic system itself. Yet it is also possible that the public effectively distinguishes press actors – many of whom suffer from low prestige in the public's mind – from the freedom that those very actors exercise. If the latter is the case, the democratic system may go on functioning properly even as the Fourth Estate's reputation continues its unfortunate slide.

Although the subject of some heated debate in recent years, David Easton's "Systems Theory" approach to understanding the dynamics of public support for a political system provides a useful framework by which to begin this discussion. As we noted previously, our purpose in using systems theory in this limited manner is *not* to resurrect the model to offer an overarching explanation of the political forces at work in this context. Rather, it is to provide some perspective on the role that public opinion can play in buttressing or undermining democratic institutions. Before returning to the central debate over the rationality and intrinsic worth of public opinion, let us first consider what is at stake in the debate itself.

Easton and Dennis (1969) define political support as ". . . feelings of trust, confidence or affection and their opposites that persons may direct toward some object" (p. 57). They draw an important distinction between two conceptualizations of support. One refers to the opinions and attitudes an individual might have regarding a particular institution, actor, or set of events. This conceptualization is termed "specific support." Support is specific if it is provided in return for satisfactory outputs. The second notion of support is based on a more general affinity for the underlying system and set of rules governing the system, and it is termed "diffuse support." Easton and Dennis write that "Diffuse support is . . . the generalized trust and confidence that members invest in various objects of the system as ends in themselves" (pp. 62–3).

While specific support is more sensitive to the current political environment, diffuse support begins to develop at a very early age and is less reactive to particular events. The early literature on political socialization, in the 1960s and 1970s, demonstrated that generalized positive feelings about the political system are developed early in life and are quite resistant to change (Schwartz, 1975). Dennis (1973) also found that political support develops early and that this development is largely devoid of experience and particular information. This early positive development provides the basic requisite levels of diffuse support that maintain individuals' affinity for the political system through the course of their respective lives. Easton and Dennis (1973), Jennings and Niemi (1974), and Miller (1974) do note, however, that diffuse support (while quite stable) may erode over the life cycle. These "primacy" theorists argue, however, that the early developed feelings of trust that provide for high levels of diffuse system support are generally resistant to change as a result of specific events.

Easton and Dennis provide an equally important rationale for distinguishing between these two political support concepts: "The peculiar quality of this kind of attachment [diffuse support] to an object is that it is not contingent on any quid pro quo; it is offered unconditionally" (p. 63). They suggest that higher levels of diffuse support might provide stability for the political system to persist over time: "Diffuse support forms a reservoir upon which a system typically draws in times of crisis, such as depressions, wars, and internal conflicts, when perceived benefits may recede to their lowest ebb" (p. 63).

The theoretical importance of fluctuations in specific and diffuse support is significant, if controversial. Maintenance of sufficient levels of diffuse support for the system may be crucial to the stability of a governmental system. Levels of specific support, on the other hand, may – and in fact are expected to – ebb and flow to varying degrees. Relating this model to the central thesis of this book is useful. We are concerned here about the diffuse level of support that the public has in a core principle underlying the U.S. political system: freedom of the press.

We have documented in the previous chapter that public support for particular actors (journalists and media professionals) and particular institutions (the news media) has declined over the long haul. The decline may be part of the ebb and flow of specific support. But this decline may also be so long term and so severe that the underlying diffuse support in the values associated with freedom of the press may be affected. In short, the reservoir of good will that the public maintains for freedom of the press could be reaching dangerously low levels, thereby compromising the legitimacy of the American political system. Certainly that has been the conclusion reached by numerous legal experts (Richards, 1998; Sanford, 1999) based on anecdotal evidence. We address this question more systematically in Chapter 4.

Easton and Dennis (1969) and Easton (1975) also propose an important distinction between three different objects of political support that offers some guidance as we assess the status of freedom of the press vis-à-vis the public, the political community, the regime, and authorities. The political community is the part ". . . of the political system that we can identify as a collection of persons who share a division of labor" (1969, p. 58). Examples of the political community are Congress, political parties, and the press. The "regime" is ". . . the constitutional order in the very broadest sense of the term. It refers to the underlying goals that members of the system pursue, the norms and rules of the game through which they conduct their political business, and the formal and informal structures of authority that arrange who is to do what in the system" (p. 59). Finally, "authorities" are those persons ". . . in the political system in whom the primary responsibility is lodged for taking care of the daily routines of a political system. In a democratic system we describe them as the elected representatives, [and] other public officials . . ." (p. 60). Members of the news media generally fall into the "authorities" category.

These distinctions between the objects of support are useful in addressing our central hypothesis. Diffuse support is driven by opinions about the broadest of these objects – namely, the regime. On the other hand, specific support is based more on opinions about the political community and authorities. In the context of our thesis, the regime relates to "freedom of the press" as an underlying goal of the system that members of the system pursue. In Easton's words, freedom of the press is part of the "norms and rules of the game" through which political business is conducted as part of the "constitutional order in its broadest sense." Diffuse support for freedom of the press guides the members' orientation toward the political system. The reservoir of good will toward the values of freedom of the press provides stability in the system and contributes to the system's legitimacy. An important focus of the analysis presented in this book, then, is on diffuse support for freedom of the press.

On the other hand, when the object of opinion relates to authorities in the press – such as journalists, news commentators, or news media executives, or the part of the political community that collectively shares the division of labor related to the function of the press, such as news media organizations – then the level of support being measured is *specific* support. As systems theory notes, low levels of specific support do not represent threats to the stability of the system. The ebb and flow of specific support is expected. "Bombarding events," in the words of Easton, are likely to drain specific support for the political community and authorities. But the buffer zone, he argues, or reservoir of good will, maintains order and stability. *The implication is that low support for the news media as an institution and members of the news media in particular does not necessarily represent trouble for the system.* Bombarding events such as public dissatisfaction with the coverage of the Clinton-Lewinsky or O. J. Simpson trial stories might be expected to lower *specific support*, but the reservoir of good will built up for the freedom of the press should protect the system's stability during these more "troubled" times.

However, the systems theory framework also advances an important caveat about the diffuse/specific support distinction. The two levels of support are not mutually exclusive and thus not unaffected by each other. The buffer zone established by diffuse support, if high, is likely to mitigate against severe drops in specific support for an object. For example, if diffuse support for freedom of the press is high, then a bombarding event, such as a Supreme Court ruling that it is legal for individuals to place sexually explicit material on the Internet, may provide a buffer against severe drops in specific support. Likewise, a series of bombarding events leading to drops in specific support may, over the long haul, drain the reservoir of good will. Thus one important question we ask is whether the long decline in confidence in the news media and journalists, fueled by a long series of bombarding events, has drained the reservoir of good will that the public holds for freedom of the press. Certainly it is also possible that the reservoir of good will for freedom of the press remains strong and sturdy despite popular dissatisfaction with the performance of the contemporary media.

THE "RATIONALITY" DEBATE: A MODERN APPROACH TO PUBLIC OPINION

This book attempts to address an important question that has dogged political observers and political scientists for years – namely, how coherent is public thinking when it comes to democratic governance and principles, as well as to issues pertaining to the constitutional rights of individuals in a free society? Earlier works by Samuel Stouffer (1955), Prothro and Grigg (1960), and McCloskey (1964) argued that while the public supported broad conceptions of constitutional rights, it was often unwilling to extend those rights to specific controversial situations. During the same period, Philip Converse (1964) concluded that the American public lacked much ability to think ideologically or with a constrained, logical approach. Moreover, popular support for the Supreme Court's controversial opinions (to the extent it existed at all) was driven by certain elites and activists (Adamany and Grossman, 1983).

To be sure, questions about the ability of the public to contribute meaningfully to debates about issues or democratic principles were asked long before the 1950s and 1960s. Aristotle and Plato raised such concerns centuries ago, and the misgivings many of the U.S. Constitution's authors felt about the abilities of the public were apparent in *The Federalist Papers*. Alexander Hamilton in particular expressed serious concerns that the public was easily and dangerously swayed to action – action that jeopardized basic principles of minority rights. He and many of his contemporaries viewed the masses as uninformed, easily manipulated, and prone to making decisions on the basis of emotions rather than on disciplined thinking. Hamilton's concerns about the public manifested themselves in constitutional mechanisms such as the electoral college and the election of U.S. senators by state legislatures. The first empirical research on these issues, conducted by Converse and others in the 1950s and 1960s, seemed to confirm the worst fears of these earlier theorists.

A new school of thought emerged, however, to challenge the question of the public's political sophistication and offer a more optimistic view of its capabilities. Scholars of this new school have not only applied more advanced methodological techniques to address the question of mass public sophistication, but they have also reconceptualized approaches to understanding the role the masses play in democracy. A pioneer in this line of thinking was V. O. Key Jr., who, in arguing for a "responsible electorate," asserted that "voters are not fools." Acknowledging that the public often does seem to act in odd ways, Key concluded that the electorate behaves "about as rationally and responsibly as we should expect," given the clarity of the alternatives presented to it and the character of the information available to it (1966). Unfortunately, researchers concerned with the public's orientation toward constitutional rights failed to specifically acknowledge all of Key's concerns. As mentioned earlier, Prothro and Grigg found that while the public strongly supported basic rights at the broad abstract level, it largely failed in its ability to translate support for those rights when spelled out in concrete terms.

Stouffer, as well as McCloskey and Brill, also argued that the mass public exhibited low levels of appreciation for and tolerance of the application of individual rights in concrete situations.

Still, during the final decade of the twentieth century, there emerged some indication that many of the old assumptions about public attitudes might finally be giving way. Specifically, some scholars have begun to express a healthy new brand of skepticism – not about public attitudes themselves, but about the way that survey research into public opinion is often conducted. From their own review of survey data on the subject, Joel Grossman and Charles Epp (1991) found that mass attitudes toward civil liberties afforded to others are

essentially passive and extremely passive constructs, less coherent principles or prologues to action than often hasty responses to harried survey researchers. Few of these attitudes are well enough formed, or strongly enough held, absent other stimuli, to actually lead to active support for, or opposition to, the rights of others (p. 27).

Their reference to "responses to harried survey researchers" is especially insightful. In fact, much of the revisionist literature on the rationality of the public offers methodological explanations for why surveys may routinely understate the abilities of the public. Zaller (1992) argues that measurement error often inhibits the ability of social researchers to gauge effectively what is really in peoples' heads.

In addition to these methodological problems, revisionists like Key have offered other reasons to think that the public is quite rational. Shafer and Claggett (1995) and Daniel Yankelovich (1991) assert that while knowledge and understanding of specific policy details tend to be low, the masses do possess an underlying value system that guides issue preferences. Such a value system enables the public to understand the principles of the political world and, as Yankelovich puts it, "come to public judgment" on important issues.

Yet it was Benjamin Page and Robert Shapiro (1992) who offered perhaps the most compelling evidence in favor of a rational public. Analyzing responses to thousands of survey items on national polls from 1935 to 1990, they demonstrate empirically that public opinion is rational in nature – at least when examining opinion in the aggregate, rather than at the individual level. Acknowledging that Americans know little about government and policy specifics, they find that "collective responses make sense . . . and they form meaningful patterns consistent with a set of underlying beliefs and values." They argue that collective opinion is solid and meaningful despite the fact that individual opinions are shaky and often nonexistent. Thus the underlying logic of a well-formed value system, along with the inevitability of measurement and random error, helps to explain why the public employs a rational approach to policy preferences.

This book presents additional evidence that the collective opinion of the masses offers strong support for a rational public on issues related to free expression. Nearly a quarter-century ago, Austin Sarat (1977) found that Americans endorse ideals of equal treatment in society. Building on Sarat's discovery, we argue that Americans bring a rational approach not only to the ideals of free expression but also to the application of those free expression rights by the media, in the form of free press rights. Our argument is based on an examination of the collective opinion of the American public on the application of free press rights. Our findings ultimately support the revisionists' argument that the mass public does exhibit the structure and qualities of a rational approach to thinking about civil liberties.

Along the way to reaching that conclusion, we examine in considerable detail the following questions about public support for freedom of the press:

- What do Americans know about the basic free expression right of free press, and how important do they perceive that right to be in the functioning of their political system? Do Americans exhibit sufficient levels of knowledge and awareness of freedom of the press to adequately exercise their rights?
- What is the level of support for freedom of the press in the United States today, and how has this support level changed? Do Americans distinguish between support for the First Amendment in general and support for freedom of the press? Is the current level of support for press freedoms at a level that endangers the stability of the political system, or is the reservoir of good will toward freedom of the press high enough to conclude that the political system is not in danger?
- When the public is presented with particular circumstances that place some strain on attitudes about freedom of the press, does support for that liberty drop off or remain high? In other words, does diffuse support for free press include concrete as well as abstract support?
- What are the sources of support for free press rights within the general public? Do factors such as level of education, political knowledge and involvement, age, and political ideology have an effect on levels of support for freedom of the press?
- Is American support for free press "unconditional," or does the nature of the medium influence whether or not the public is willing to support an extension of free press rights? Strong support levels

should promote a willingness to extend free press rights across all forms of media (e.g., newspapers, electronic, Internet, etc.). Yet with the proliferation of news media outlets (e.g., traditional ones such as newspapers and TV as well as electronic media such as the Internet and talk radio), have Americans begun to distinguish between those media which should be allowed to exercise the rights of a free press and those that should not be allowed to do so?

• Similarly, does the public's support for press rights extend equally to specific news sources, or does the public distinguish among the sources to which it is willing to extend rights? Again, the changing nature of news has resulted in more traditional, respected sources (such as the *New York Times*, *Newsweek*, and the network news broadcasts) on the one hand, and the more sensational, tabloid, and controversial sources (such as *Hustler*, "The Jerry Springer Show," and "Inside Edition") on the other. Are Americans willing to extend the same levels of freedom to all sources, or to just a few? If the public does differentiate among news sources in its willingness to extend free press rights, what are the implications for the status of press freedom in our society?

RESEARCH DESIGN AND METHODOLOGY

To examine public attitudes about the freedom of the press and explore the foregoing hypotheses relating to how these opinions may negatively affect the U.S. political system, we draw primarily on two national surveys conducted in 1997 and 1999. These surveys were conducted by the Center for Survey Research and Analysis (CSRA) at the University of Connecticut and were designed specifically to explore contemporary public opinion about the First Amendment, with particular focus on freedom of the press and freedom of speech. The surveys were funded in large part by grants from the First Amendment Center, an operating program of the Freedom Forum.

The two main surveys were conducted in July 1997 and March 1999. (A more limited, follow-up survey was also conducted during the spring of 2000.) Each of these surveys included a national random-digit-dial sample of 1,000 adults (age eighteen and older). The survey instruments were developed by CSRA and the First Amendment Center. The following is a full description of sampling design, fieldwork experience, sampling error for the surveys, design of the survey instruments, and core variables drawn from the data sets that are used as independent variables for analysis throughout subsequent chapters of this book.

Sample Design

The University of Connecticut's CSRA follows procedures in sampling and data processing that are designed to minimize error in its results.

For the sampling procedure, we used a variation of random-digit dialing; working residential "blocks" were identified with the aid of published directories. These exchanges were chosen in a modified stratified procedure based on the proportion of the theoretical universe residing in the geographic area covered by each published directory. Thus, in general, if 10 percent of the universe lives in the area covered by a directory, 10 percent of the exchanges will be chosen from that area. The universe for the First Amendment project was the adult non-institutionalized population of the contiguous forty-eight states who were eighteen years of age and older. The geographic distribution in sampling was based on estimates of the distribution derived from the census figures for towns.

Once "working blocks" were identified, one telephone number was generated at random for each block. A household was given five distinct opportunities to be contacted before a substitution was made for it. Once it was determined that the household did, in fact, contain an eligible respondent, a random selection – unbiased on age and on sex among the eligible respondents – was made. Should that person not be the one with whom the original conversation was taking place, he or she was called to the telephone. The definition of household used was "all adults eighteen years of age and older who lived in the dwelling place." Such institutions as college dormitories, prisons, and the like were omitted.

Fieldwork

All interviewing for this project was conducted at the University of Connecticut CSRA's telephone center. Interviewing for the 1997 survey was conducted by telephone between July 17 and August 1, 1997. Interviewing for the initial 1999 survey was conducted by telephone between February 26 and March 24, 1999. We utilized a Computer Assisted Telephone Interviewing (CATI) system to conduct the interviewing. When using the CATI system, questionnaires are computerized, reducing the amount of human error in the survey process. The telephone interviews took place in the evenings on weekdays, Saturday mornings and afternoons, and Sunday afternoons and evenings. This avoided a bias in selecting people only at home at certain times. If a given telephone number did not result in an interview – for whatever reason – a substitution was made for it from within the same working block (which functions as our single member "cluster"). This meant that one person's not being at home, for example, did not keep his or her cluster from being included in the sample.

Sampling Error and Survey Instrument Design

A total of 1,000 interviews with a national scientific sample of adults eighteen years of age or older was conducted for both the 1997 and 1999 surveys. Sampling error for a sample of this size is ±3% at the 95 percent level of confidence. Sampling error for subgroups (e.g., men, women, etc.) is larger.

The survey instruments for the 1997 and 1999 surveys were designed to measure public knowledge and opinion about the First Amendment generally, with particular focus on the freedoms of press and, to some extent, speech. A number of the items from the 1997 survey were repeated to measure change and continuity of opinion across the two-year period. Both survey instruments were pre-tested with thirty respondents. The pre-test was used to ensure that questions were understood by respondents and that response categories were appropriate.

Specifically, the design of the survey instruments was intended to achieve the following objectives:

- To measure the public perceptions of the importance of freedom of the press and its relative importance compared with other constitutionally guaranteed rights.
- To understand public awareness of freedom of the press as a right that is guaranteed by the Constitution and compare level of awareness of freedom of the press with that of other First Amendment rights.
- To examine the level of knowledge the public exhibits with respect to what freedoms the press has in particular areas and to measure public knowledge of specific contemporary topics related to free press issues.
- To gauge diffuse support for freedom of the press and other free expression rights at two levels: abstract support for the broad concept of free press, and concrete support for the public's willingness to adhere to press freedoms, even under sometimes offensive circumstances.
- To evaluate the public mind regarding the current status of freedom of press in the United States – whether or not the press has the right amount of freedom, too much, or too little; and compare this opinion with that regarding other expressive freedoms.
- To ascertain if and the extent to which the public distinguishes between the type of news medium when thinking about the level of freedom it is willing to extend to the press. Do members of the public differentiate between what freedoms they are willing to extend to TV versus newspaper versus the Internet, and so on?
- To ascertain if and the extent to which the public distinguishes between press organizations within a news medium or individual journalists when thinking about the level of freedom it is willing to

afford. For example, does the public distinguish between the rights extended to "ABC News" and "The Jerry Springer Show"?

The questions asked in the 1997 and 1999 surveys are included in the appendix.

In addition to addressing these objectives, the survey instruments gathered background information on respondents to facilitate population subgroup analysis of the data. These "background" items form the basis for a number of independent variables we use in our analysis of the findings. The independent variables drawn from these data sets that are used throughout this book are:

- Gender (male, female)
- Age (eighteen to twenty-nine, thirty to forty-four, forty-five to sixty-one, sixty-two or older)
- An individual's main news source (e.g., newspaper, TV, radio, etc.)
- Access to and use of the Internet
- Level of education (high school graduate, some college but no degree, college degree)
- Ethnicity (white, African-American, Latino, other)
- Family income (under $30,000, $30,000 to $50,000, $50,000 to $75,000, over $75,000)
- Religious affiliation (Catholic, Protestant, Jewish, other)
- Religious service attendance (at least once/week, at least once/month, less than once/month, not at all)
- Political party identification (Democrat, Republican, independent)
- Political ideology (liberal, moderate, conservative)
- First Amendment education (whether or not the respondent ever had a course in high school or college that provided instruction on First Amendment issues)
- First Amendment knowledge (This is an index from a series of six questions asking if, under current law, Americans have the legal right to perform a certain act. For each correct answer given, a respondent received a score of one. The possible range of overall scores for an individual was zero (no answer correct) to six (all answers correct). Ranges of scores were grouped into categories in the following manner: (1) Low Knowledge: overall score between 0 and 2, (2) Medium-Low Knowledge: score of 3, (3) Medium-High Knowledge: score of 4, (4) High Knowledge: score between 5 and 6).
- Political participation (this is an index from a series of seven questions asking whether or not a person participated in politics in the past year. For each "Yes," a respondent was given a score of one; conversely, each "No" answer resulted in a zero. The possible range

of overall scores for an individual was zero (having performed none
of the activities asked) to seven (having done all of the activities
asked). Ranges of scores were grouped into categories in the
following manner: (1) Low Political Participation: overall score
between 0 and 2, (2) Medium Political Participation: score between
3 and 4, (3) High Political Participation: score between 5 and 7.

In the chapters that follow, we use these independent variables to
examine how various segments of the public are consistent or different
in their levels of knowledge and in their opinions about the First Amendment and in particular freedom of the press. The research we conducted
provides a strong empirical basis on which to assess the status of freedom
of the press in the United States at the turn of the century. The survey
instruments were specifically designed to address the hypotheses advanced earlier in this chapter and to evaluate the integrity of freedom of
the press. In the next chapter, we review our findings related to citizens'
knowledge of and engagement in First Amendment and freedom of the
press issues, and in Chapter 4 we tackle head-on questions relating to
the nature of diffuse support for press freedoms.

3

What Americans Know About
the Freedom of the Press

Rights of free expression serve as the cornerstone of liberty in the U.S. political culture. While no such rights were included in the Constitution as it was adopted in 1789, some of the framers argued for the incorporation of free expression rights at the outset, and they successfully secured inclusion of those rights two years later in the First Amendment to the Constitution. Democratic theorists and more casual observers of the American political system agree that free expression rights provide the basis for the free flow of information that the public needs in a free society to make important electoral choices and other decisions (Murphy, 1991). Free expression rights also facilitate a robust debate on policy issues and assist the public and policymakers alike in forming opinions based on a thorough exploration of issues and positions.

As we argued in Chapter 1, the most salient roles the press serves in exercising its freedoms are as (1) watchdog of public officials and institutions, (2) an important channel through which political leaders can reach the public, and, occasionally, (3) an advocate of the public will. Given the importance of these functions, one might anticipate a high level of support for these freedoms (resulting from political socialization) (see Jennings and Niemi, 1983), as well as a high level of awareness and recognition of those rights by citizens. Because the American political culture endorses and encourages free-spirited political debate and participative democracy, one would naturally expect the mass public to express at least some awareness and understanding of these core rights.

In this chapter, we explore the American mass public's awareness, understanding, and knowledge of the freedom of the press for several reasons. First, we would expect that the masses are both knowledgeable about and appreciative of such a core liberty in the U.S. political system. Second, we know from prior public opinion research that opinions formed on the basis of greater awareness and knowledge are less susceptible to radical shifts (Zaller, 1992; Delli Carpini and Keeter, 1996;

Neuman, 1991). Stated simply, a mass public that is more knowledge-able about this liberty is less likely to hold back its support of those rights. Finally, awareness and knowledge of free expression rights such as those embodied in freedom of the press are important precursors to the exercise of those liberties. If the public is encouraged to exercise liberty to promote democracy, it must know what liberty is at its dis-posal. In short, knowledge of liberty may well contribute to the exercise of liberty – and so in order to understand opinion and the exercise of freedom of the press, we need to consider the level of awareness and knowledge that exists concerning the freedom of the press.

This chapter explores public awareness and knowledge of freedom of the press on a number of dimensions. First, we broadly examine the public's orientation toward the First Amendment as a whole by exam-ining levels of formal education on First Amendment issues, how closely members of the public follow First Amendment issues, and what they think about how much First Amendment freedoms are appreciated. Next, we examine the public's recognition of the freedom of the press in particular as an important liberty in American society, and public aware-ness of this liberty as a right that is guaranteed by the First Amendment. We also examine the relative importance Americans assign to freedom of the press, as compared with other freedoms set forth in the U.S. Constitution. Finally, we explore the specific knowledge Americans possess regarding the application of free press rights in the contempo-rary United States.

PUBLIC AWARENESS AND RECOGNITION OF THE FIRST AMENDMENT

Freedom of the press is one of the critical self-expression rights guaran-teed by the First Amendment. As part of that amendment's core set of rights, it is useful to understand Americans' general orientations toward the full package of rights guaranteed by the First Amendment prior to a more comprehensive examination of orientations toward freedom of the press specifically. In this section we review data related to Ameri-can awareness, recognition, and knowledge of the First Amendment generally.

We begin with the finding that the public maintains a high degree of affection for the First Amendment. After respondents in our sample were read the text of the First Amendment and then asked whether or not they would vote to approve or not approve this Amendment if they were voting today, fully 93 percent said they would vote to approve it.[1] While

[1] This finding is drawn from the July 1997 CSRA survey.

such a high favorable response to this question is primed in part by the social desirability of the response, we also detected strong public affection for the First Amendment based on the following item: "Based on your own feelings about the First Amendment, please tell me whether you agree or disagree with the following statement: The First Amendment goes too far in the rights it guarantees." Fully two-thirds of the sample in the 1999 survey disagreed with this statement, with as many as 45 percent "strongly" disagreeing. Even when we posed the question from a negative reference point (thus reducing the potential problem of the socially desirable response), we still detected significant affection for the First Amendment.

To what extent is this affection based on knowledge and recognition of the First Amendment itself? One important factor contributing to the public's knowledge of the First Amendment is the level of formal education that Americans have received on First Amendment issues. In both the 1997 and 1999 CSRA First Amendment surveys, we asked respondents whether they had ever taken classes in high school or college that dealt with First Amendment issues. In both surveys we found that about half (52 percent in 1999 and 51 percent in 1997) indicated that they had taken such courses at some point in their life. We asked those who said they had had such a course to indicate the level at which they'd had taken them. Two-thirds of this group responded that they'd had coursework in First Amendment issues in high school, 56 percent said they'd had First Amendment coursework in college, and 16 percent said they'd had it in grades prior to high school.

There are important differences across several demographic groups in the degree to which they received formal training in First Amendment issues. As one might expect, those with more education – those who have had a greater opportunity to partake in courses where First Amendment instruction is offered – are more likely to have benefited from formal training. Specifically, 67 percent of those with a college degree say they have had some coursework in First Amendment issues, compared with 62 percent of those with some college experience but not a degree and 40 percent of those with only a high school education. Clearly, higher education promotes formal training in First Amendment issues.

There also exists a clear relationship between age and coursework on First Amendment issues (see Figure 3.1), with younger people much more likely to acknowledge having taken such courses. Specifically, 67 percent of eighteen- to twenty-nine-year-olds, 54 percent of thirty- to forty-four-year-olds, 51 percent of forty-five- to sixty-one-year-olds, and only 30 percent of those sixty-two or older have ever had such formal

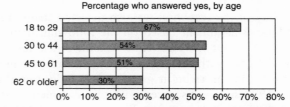

Figure 3.1. Coursework on First Amendment issues. **"To the best of your recollec-tion, have you ever taken classes in either school or college that dealt with First Amendment freedoms?"** (Source: CSRA University of Connecticut Survey, 1999.)

coursework.[2] Even though it may be the case that older individuals simply find it more difficult to remember having had such coursework, the strength of the relationship suggests that contemporary education in the United States has increasingly focused on First Amendment topics.

If about half of the American public has had formal training in First Amendment issues, is that a positive or negative reflection on the public's preparedness? How well has the educational system performed in teaching Americans about free-expressive freedoms? Later in this chapter, we review the public opinion data on public knowledge of freedom of the press and other liberties to evaluate the intellectual capital of Americans in this area. At this point, however, it is useful to review what the public thinks about the American educational system's effectiveness in preparing students on First Amendment issues. In the 1997 survey, we asked our national sample the following question: "Overall, how would you rate the job that the American education system does in teaching students about First Amendment freedoms – excellent, good, only fair, or poor?"

Figure 3.2 shows that the public is not very enthusiastic about the performance of the educational system in this area. Only 4 percent offer a rating of "excellent," and an additional 26 percent say the educational system is doing a "good" job of teaching students about the First Amend-ment. The large majority of citizens give it a negative performance rating of either "poor" (22 percent) or "only fair" (41 percent). From the per-spective of the public, improvements are needed in the formal education of Americans on the First Amendment.

---

[2] Naturally, the educational system in the United States, with its focus on issues related to First Amendment rights, has undergone substantial changes over the past several decades. The Warren Court's attention to these issues in the 1960s surely increased the extent to which modern curricula incorporate instruction on Bill of Rights issues. Most older Americans, especially those in the sixty-two-or-over age group, likely received their education prior to such changes.

Figure 3.2. Rating of educational system's performance in First Amendment instruction. "Overall, how would you rate the job that the American educational system does in teaching students about First Amendment freedoms – excellent, good, only fair, or poor?" (Source: CSRA University of Connecticut Survey, 1997.)

Attentiveness to First Amendment Liberties

The extent to which the public pays attention to First Amendment issues in the first place and its appreciation of free expression rights generally are also important factors contributing to knowledge of the First Amendment. The more attention people pay to news reports related to free expression rights, the higher and more stable will be the levels of public support for those rights.

Generally, most Americans indicate that they do pay attention to issues involving First Amendment rights. When asked, "How closely do you pay attention to issues involving the First Amendment's freedoms of speech, press, religion, assembly, and petition?" more than eight in ten say they pay either "a lot" (39 percent) or "some" (45 percent) attention. Only 15 percent say they pay "only a little" or no attention to these issues. At least in terms of self-expressions of attentiveness to First Amendment issues, Americans appear to be fairly engaged.

In addition to this general question about attentiveness to First Amendment issues, our 1997 and 1999 surveys asked respondents about attentiveness to some specific free expression issues that were being publicly debated during the time of the surveys. These items provide more specific measures of public attentiveness to First Amendment issues. One such measure was taken in the July 1997 survey, about one month after the U.S. Supreme Court's landmark ruling concerning Internet rights. In *Reno v. ACLU*,[3] the Court, in the course of invalidating a federal law regulating obscenity on the Internet, ruled that material on that new medium enjoyed virtually the same level of First Amendment protection

---

[3] 521 U.S. 844 (1997).

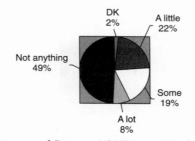

Figure 3.3. Public awareness of *Reno v. ACLU* case. "To the best of your recollection, have you read or heard anything about a recent U.S. Supreme Court ruling regarding the Internet?" IF YES: "How much have you read or head – a lot, some, or just a little?" (Source: CSRA University of Connecticut Survey, 1997.)

as printed material such as books and newspapers. This ruling was highly publicized and debated on the airwaves and in print, and the public had ample opportunity to become exposed to this specific issue. Still, we found in 1997 that just half of the public (49 percent) was aware of this ruling, while the other half (49 percent) had not read or heard anything about it.[4] Among the 49 percent who claimed to be aware of the decision, 8 percent said they'd read or heard "a lot" about it, 19 percent had "some" familiarity with it, and 22 percent knew just "a little." (See Figure 3.3.)

Similar findings arose from a question on the 1999 survey with regard to awareness of the "Nuremberg Files" case, a highly publicized federal district court verdict concerning the publication of abortion doctors' names and addresses in the form of "wanted" posters on an Internet site. Figure 3.4 shows that 44 percent of the public had read or heard nothing about the case, while 56 percent were familiar with it. Among the 56 percent who were aware, 11 percent said they knew "a lot," 21 percent knew "some," and 24 percent were only "a little" familiar.

Our findings on public awareness of highly publicized free press issues, then, indicates that about half of all Americans are at least modestly engaged in following these issues – far less than the 85 percent who claim to follow First Amendment topics as a whole.[5]

---

[4] The question used to measure awareness of this Supreme Court ruling does not refer to the *Reno v. ACLU* case directly, in order to capture positive responses from those aware of the decision generally but unaware of the case name.

[5] Another survey that CSRA conducted in 1995, immediately after the jury award in the Food Lion case, found that 51 percent of the adult American public was aware of the case, providing further evidence that the attentive public on First Amendment free press issues constitutes about half the population.

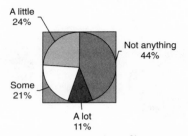

Figure 3.4. Public awareness of the "Nuremberg files" case. "Recently, a federal jury ruled that a Web site featuring 'wanted' posters listing abortion doctors' names and addresses amounted to death threats and therefore ordered the site's authors to pay damages. How much have you heard about this – a lot, some, a little, or nothing at all?" (Source: CSRA, University of Connecticut, 1999.)

Appreciation for First Amendment Liberties

A public sense of appreciation for the values and rights embodied in the First Amendment provides yet another indicator of awareness and recognition of self-expression rights. Appreciating these rights and recognizing their role and existence may result in an increased propensity to exercise First Amendment rights, and so our surveys attempted to measure public appreciation and awareness of them. Our findings on several measures of this dimension, as shown in Figure 3.5, are consistent: People generally believe that Americans do not fully appreciate First Amendment freedoms and tend to take them for granted.

For example, three-quarters of the public agreed with the following statement: "Americans don't appreciate First Amendment freedoms the way they ought to." Fully 47 percent strongly agreed with this statement, and another 29 percent mildly agreed.[6] In addition, nearly nine in ten Americans (87 percent) feel that the rights guaranteed by the First Amendment are taken for granted by most people, and more than half (54 percent) admit that these rights are something that they themselves tend to take for granted.[7]

PUBLIC AWARENESS AND RECOGNITION OF FREEDOM OF THE PRESS

In this section, we examine public awareness and recognition specifically of freedom of the press. First, we look at the public's ability to identify freedom of the press as one of the particular freedoms that are included

---

[6] This item was included on the 1997 survey.
[7] These items were included on the 1999 survey.

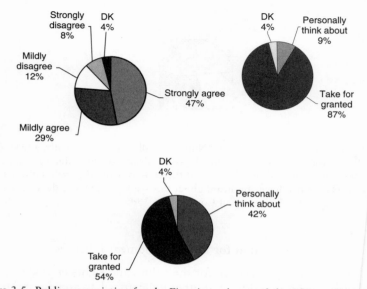

Figure 3.5. Public appreciation for the First Amendment. (*left*) "Please tell me if you agree or disagree with the following statement: Americans don't appreciate First Amendment freedoms the way they ought to." (*bottom*) "Are the rights guaranteed by the First Amendment something you personally think about or are they something you take for granted?" (*right*) "What about most people in the United States – do you think the rights guaranteed by the First Amendment are something people specifically think about or are they something they take for granted?" (Source: CSRA University of Connecticut Survey, 1999.)

in the First Amendment. Second, we identify the proportion of Americans who identify freedom of the press as an important freedom in American society and compare those findings with those associated with other specific rights identified as most important.

The Salience of Free Press Rights

As a simple measure of awareness, we asked our samples of Americans in both 1997 and 1999 if they could name any of the specific rights guaranteed by the First Amendment. This question measures salience and unaided awareness of the various freedoms in the First Amendment. Table 3.1 shows public awareness of freedom of the press and compares it with public awareness of the other First Amendment freedoms.

In both 1997 and 1999, about one in ten Americans was consistently able to name "freedom of the press" as one of the rights guaranteed by

Table 3.1. Awareness of the Freedoms in the First Amendment

"As you may know, the First Amendment is part of the U.S. Constitution. Can you name any of the specific rights that are guaranteed by the First Amendment?"

	1997	1999
Freedom of the press	11%	12%
Freedom of speech	49	44
Freedom of religion	21	13
Right of assembly/association	10	8
Right to petition	2	2
Other mention	7	6
Cannot name any	37	39

Note: Percentages represent the number of respondents who named each freedom unaided.

Source: CSRA University of Connecticut Surveys, 1997 and 1999.

the First Amendment. Awareness of freedom of the press is far lower than awareness of freedom of speech (of which free press rights are technically a component), and less than freedom of religion. One factor may be the 1997 Supreme Court decision on freedom of religion (*City of Boerne v. Flores*[8]), which received considerable attention from the media. The change in Table 3.1 concerning awareness of freedom of religion from 1997 to 1999 may be partially explained by the media's attention to that decision. The right of assembly has about the same level of unaided awareness as freedom of the press. Americans are least familiar with the right to petition, a largely meaningless right today.

There are some demographic differences in awareness of freedom of the press. Men (14 percent) are slightly more likely than women (9 percent) to exhibit awareness of this right, and those with higher family incomes are more likely to identify freedom of the press as being part of the First Amendment.

[8] 521 U.S. 507 (1997). In *City of Boerne,* the Court considered the constitutionality of the widely popular Religious Freedom Restoration Act of 1993, which attempted to provide a stronger claim or defense in court to any person whose religious exercise had been substantially burdened by the government. In striking down the RFRA as unconstitutional, the Court found that Congress had exceeded its authority under the Constitution to provide such a remedy.

Perceived Importance of Freedom of the Press as a Liberty

To what extent does the American public believe that the freedom of the press is an important freedom in their society, and how does the perceived importance of free press rights compare with the perceived importance of other rights? Our surveys addressed these questions in two ways. First, we asked an open-ended response question at the start of the survey interviews that asked people to name the rights or freedoms they felt were most important in American society. Respondents were probed to offer as many rights and freedom as they wanted to. Responses to this item provide a measure of "unaided" recognition of the perceived importance of specific rights, including that of freedom of the press. Second, we offered respondents a series of different rights that are protected by the Constitution and asked how important those rights are. This method provides a measure of "aided" recognition of the perceived importance of specific rights, including freedom of the press. The unaided measure provides a sense of "top of mind" importance or salience of the right. The aided measure forces respondents to think about the specific freedom and gauges reaction to it.

Table 3.2 indicates that freedom of the press does not receive a high level of unaided recognition as an important right among the general public. In both the 1997 and 1999 surveys, only about one in twenty mentioned freedom of the press as one of the important rights in American society. In fact, several other freedoms are more frequently mentioned than freedom of the press.

The right that obtains the single highest level of perceived importance (on an unaided basis) is freedom of speech, mentioned by half of the respondents in both surveys. Freedom of speech clearly is the most salient of freedoms guaranteed by the Constitution from the perspective of the mass public. About one in five Americans mentions either freedom of religion or freedom from religion as among the most important rights in our society – a level much higher than that for freedom of the press. Also, a significantly higher number of Americans mention the right to bear arms as an important right than the number who mention freedom of the press. The increase in those mentioning the "right to bear arms" may well be the result of the numerous "school shooting" incidents that occurred between the 1997 and 1999 surveys. Those incidents, and public discussions about gun control that followed, may have mobilized support for the right to bear arms among those individuals to whom this right is important.

Interestingly, the percentage that mentioned freedom of the press on the unaided measure is fairly consistent across all demographic groups, including gender, age, income, education, race, party identification, and

Table 3.2. "Unaided" Perceived Importance of
Various Rights

"As you know, the U.S. Constitution provides citizens
many rights and freedoms. Are there any particular rights
or freedoms that you feel are most important to
American society?"

	1997	1999
Freedom of the press	5%	6%
Freedom of speech	50	50
Freedom to practice religion	14	13
Freedom not to practice religion	5	5
Right to bear arms	9	14
Freedom of assembly/association	4	4
Right to petition	1	2
Right to fair trial	2	3
Right to privacy	1	3
Freedom from unreasonable searches	1	1
Other mentions	11	14
Can't name any	30	24

Note: Percentages represent those who mentioned a specific
right.
Source: CSRA University of Connecticut Surveys, 1997 and
1999.

self-expressed political ideology. No significant differences were found
across any of these groups. One might expect, for example, that those
with more education are more likely to mention free press as a right.
However, there are no differences across levels of education groups. One
might also expect that having had some formal coursework or education
on First Amendment issues would make one more likely to mention free
press as a right, but it does not.

By comparison, on the most salient right – freedom of speech – we
do find significant differences across some key demographic groups. For
example, 61 percent of the college educated mentioned free speech on
the unaided measure, compared with only 41 percent of those with only
a high school degree. Fifty-nine percent of eighteen- to twenty-nine-year-
olds mention free speech, compared with only 44 percent of senior citizens. And those who had formal coursework on First Amendment issues
(58 percent) were more likely than those without (42 percent) to mention
free speech. So, while demographic background factors tend to influence

Table 3.3. "Aided" Perceived Importance of Various Rights

"The U.S. Constitution protects certain rights, but not everyone considers each right important. I am going to read you some rights guaranteed by the U.S. Constitution. Please tell me how important it is that you have that right. First, how important is it that the right to [ROTATE ITEMS] . . . Is it essential that you have that right, important but not essential, or not that important?"

Right to	Essential	Important	Not important
a free press	60%	33%	6%
a fair trial	86	14	0
practice the religion of your choice	81	18	1
privacy	78	21	1
free speech	72	27	1
practice no religion	66	24	9
assemble/protest/petition	56	37	7
own firearms	33	31	33

Note: Table excludes those saying "don't know."
Source: CSRA University of Connecticut Survey, 1997.

unaided recognition of free speech, unaided recognition of free press is not affected by those characteristics.

Our second approach to measuring perceived importance of freedom of the press involved the "aided" questions, as described previously. We asked respondents to indicate how important it was that Americans enjoy each of the rights listed in Table 3.3. For each of these rights, respondents were asked to indicate whether it was "essential," "important," or "not that important" to have them. The table shows that while a clear majority of Americans – 60 percent – says that the right to a free press is "essential," one-third indicates it is important but not essential, and one in twenty says that it is not important at all. Further, a number of the other rights for which we provided an aided perceived importance measure obtained higher percentages saying those freedoms are "essential." The right to a fair trial, the right to freedom of and freedom from religion, the right to freedom of speech, and the right to privacy all are viewed by more Americans as more essential rights than the freedom of the press.

PUBLIC KNOWLEDGE OF SPECIFIC FREE PRESS RIGHTS

Awareness and knowledge of First Amendment rights – including the freedom of the press – encompass more than the mere ability to name specific rights and express appreciation of them. Knowledge also features an understanding of the implementation of those rights, including knowl-

Table 3.4. Public Knowledge of What Is and What Is Not Protected by the First Amendment

"Now I'm going to read a series of statements about how people might try to exercise their rights under the First Amendment. Please tell me whether you think under current law Americans have the legal right or not to do each of the following."

	Correct answer	% correct
Do courts have the right to send reporters to jail for refusing to reveal a news source?	Yes	37%
Does the government have the right to restrict "indecent" material on the Internet?	No	40%
Do Americans have the legal right to burn the American flag as a means of political protest?	Yes	33%
Do controversial groups that hold unpopular beliefs have the legal right to demonstrate peacefully in public?	Yes	86%
Does someone have the legal right to shout "fire" in a crowded arena as a prank?	No	91%

Source: CSRA University of Connecticut Survey, 1999.

edge of the current law as it applies to the First Amendment. In our 1999 survey, we included a number of items asking respondents about the legality of exercising free expression rights under certain circumstances. In this section, we present our findings on public knowledge of actions that are either clearly protected or clearly not protected by the First Amendment under prevailing legal doctrines. We also identify which segments of society exhibit higher levels of such knowledge.

Respondents were presented with a series of actions that involved the exercise of free press rights or free speech rights. For each situation, the respondent was asked whether or not it was a legal expression protected by the First Amendment. Table 3.4 indicates the situations we presented to our sample, along with the percentage that answered correctly. The first two items in that table are related specifically to press rights. In each case, far less than a majority of Americans understood the current controlling law (i.e., whether it is "illegal" or "legal"). Specifically, 37 percent knew that courts could send reporters to jail for refusing to reveal a news source, while 54 percent thought that courts cannot do so. The remaining 9 percent admitted that they did not know the legal status of the action in question.

The effects of education and income are also apparent. Americans with higher levels of education and higher income levels are more likely to provide a correct answer. Fifty-one percent of those with a college degree knew that courts can jail reporters for not revealing a source, compared with 41 percent of those with some college experience and only 28 percent of those with no college experience. Interestingly, having taken a course that included instruction on First Amendment issues had less of an effect than overall educational attainment. Forty-two percent of those who had had First Amendment instruction answered this item correctly, as compared with 32 percent of those who had not had such instruction. The overall degree of education appears to have a greater impact on knowledge of this situation than does having had specific instruction on First Amendment issues. We also found that 46 percent of those in households earning at least $50,000 responded correctly to this item, compared with 36 percent of households earning $30,000 to $50,000 and only 28 percent of households earning under $30,000.

Additionally, there was evidence of an effect based on partisanship and, to a lesser extent, political ideology. Republicans (48 percent) are more likely than either independents (36 percent) or Democrats (31 percent) to know that reporters can be jailed for refusing to reveal a source, and political conservatives (43 percent) are more likely to correctly answer this item than are moderates (37 percent) and liberals (35 percent). This partisan and ideological effect may be the result of "wishful guessing" rather than real knowledge. (Some suspect that Republicans and conservatives – who may be more likely to subscribe to a stricter "law and order" ideology – might support the jailing of reporters for refusing to reveal sources who might help solve criminal cases.) Certainly, Republicans and conservatives might be reacting to the perceived "liberal bias" of newspapers. (See Dautrich and Hartley, 1999). Thus while Republicans are more likely to answer this item correctly, the reasons they offer may be more attitudinally based than factually based.

The second freedom of the press situation on which we queried respondents concerned the government's right to restrict "indecent" material on the Internet. The Supreme Court's *Reno v. ACLU* decision in 1997 prevented the federal government from imposing such restrictions, at least for the near future. We found that only 40 percent of Americans knew that the government did not have the right to place restrictions on Internet material, while a majority (53 percent) thought that government could in fact restrict such Internet material and 7 percent said they did not know. Once again, we find that one's overall educational attainment has an important effect on knowledge (48 percent of those with college degrees, 42 percent of those with some college experience, and 35 percent of those with no college experience answer correctly). Meanwhile, specific coursework on the First Amendment apparently had less of an effect (42 percent versus 38 percent).

For the non–free press First Amendment situations we asked about, we found the following: Only one-third of Americans know that burning the American flag as a means of political protest is constitutionally protected. These incorrect perceptions may be the result of the rather significant public discussion about flag burning that has occurred in recent years. Whenever this topic arises, most elected officials find it advantageous to criticize those who would allow the flag to be burned; such unidirectional rhetoric may have been strong enough to have convinced many in the public to believe that flag burning has become unconstitutional despite the U.S. Supreme Court's rulings to the contrary. Also, strong majorities in the general public are aware that controversial groups with unpopular beliefs have the right to demonstrate (86 percent), and that falsely shouting "fire" in a crowded theater is not protected (91 percent).

THE INFLUENCE OF KNOWLEDGE OF THE FIRST AMENDMENT ON SUPPORT

In the next chapter, we dissect possible conceptualizations of the public's support for free press rights and document existing levels of support Americans show for those rights. In this concluding section of our analysis of public knowledge of the First Amendment, however, it is instructive to assess the extent to which knowledge influences levels of support. What is the influence of knowledge of First Amendment law on overall attitudes about the First Amendment? We hypothesize that knowledge engenders greater appreciation of and tolerance for the right of Americans to exercise their First Amendment freedoms. In short, the more one knows about the First Amendment, the more one may appreciate its functional significance in and overall importance to American society. This hypothesis is consistent with the arguments made by Sullivan et al. (1978) that knowledge breeds understanding of and appreciation for fundamental properties (such as political tolerance) of democratic societies.

At the outset of this chapter, we noted that public affection for the First Amendment is relatively high, with 67 percent disagreeing with the statement "The First Amendment goes too far in the rights it guarantees." What is the impact of demonstrated knowledge of First Amendment issues on affection for the First Amendment? We would expect there to be a positive impact. As Table 3.5 shows, there is, in fact, a strong positive influence of knowledge about the First Amendment on feelings that the First Amendment does not go too far in the rights it guarantees Americans. Two-thirds of those individuals who demonstrate

Table 3.5. The Influence of Knowledge on Attitudes About the First Amendment

Percentage who strongly disagree that First Amendment goes too far *in guaranteeing rights*:

Knowledge about the First Amendment	
High	66%
High–medium	55%
Low–medium	37%
Low	31%

Note: The "Knowledge About the First Amendment" variable is built on the basis of responses to the five items presented in Table 3.4. These are items with a correct and an incorrect response. Zero or one correct response is classified as "low" knowledge; 2 correct responses are classified as "low-medium" knowledge; 3 correct responses are classified as "high-medium" knowledge; and 4 or 5 correct responses are classified as "high" knowledge

Source: CSRA University of Connecticut Survey, 1999.

a high level of knowledge about First Amendment issues strongly disagree that First Amendment rights currently go too far, compared with less than one-third of those who have low levels of knowledge. Table 3.5 provides clear evidence of a strong relationship between knowledge of the First Amendment and disagreement that the First Amendment goes too far in guaranteeing rights. Our data, then, do indeed confirm that greater levels of knowledge about First Amendment issues breed higher levels of appreciation for the First Amendment.

CONCLUSION

In this chapter, we examined public awareness and knowledge of the First Amendment, and freedom of the press in particular, on a number of levels. We discovered that about half of all Americans have taken at least one course either in high school or in college that dealt with First Amendment issues, and that more than six in ten Americans are less than enthusiastic about the overall job the educational system performs in teaching about free expression issues. The vast majority of the public says that it pays at least some attention to issues involving the First Amendment, but only about half of the public actually expresses some level of awareness of specific First Amendment topics under public debate. And many in the public, upon self-examination, admit that they take the First Amendment rights they have for granted.

In examining freedom of the press in particular, only about one in ten members of the public is able to identify this freedom as one that is part of the First Amendment, compared with about half of Americans who are able to similarly identify freedom of speech. Also, about four in ten cannot name any rights guaranteed by the First Amendment. Only about one in twenty Americans mentions, on an unaided basis, that freedom of the press is an important right guaranteed to Americans by the U.S. Constitution. By contrast, freedom to practice the religion of one's choice and the right to bear arms were each identified by more people as important constitutional freedoms than was the freedom of the press. And when individuals were specifically asked about freedom of the press, 60 percent said it was an essential right, while one-third said it was important but not essential. The rights of fair trial, religious practice, free speech, and privacy are all identified by many more Americans as "essential" in comparison with freedom of the press.

With respect to some specific applications of free press rights, Americans also tend to be fairly uninformed. For example, majorities of Americans do not know that reporters can be jailed for refusing to reveal a source, or that the government cannot restrict "indecent" material on the Internet.

We began this chapter by hypothesizing that awareness and knowledge of freedom of the press is important because it encourages the exercise of those rights (which is important for the free flow of information), and it encourages stable attitudes toward those rights, a crucial precondition to a political system's stability and legitimacy. After reviewing the data, we were heartened by some aspects of the public's awareness – at least half of the public is attentive to important First Amendment issues, and the public does largely recognize that it takes many provisions of the First Amendment for granted. Unfortunately, there are just as many areas of serious concern. Freedom of the press is not a salient freedom in the public's mind, and it is not listed by most people as a core freedom in American society. This lack of salience and perceived relative importance should give us some concern that press freedoms may be in some jeopardy. At a minimum, we might expect distrust for members of the media to translate into some reduced public support for these rights, fragile as they appear to be. In reality, however, the freedom of the press holds a far more secure position in the public's mind than these "awareness" figures might suggest. In the next chapter, we turn to an even more comprehensive analysis of support for press freedoms.

4

Public Support for the Freedom of the Press

As we argued in Chapter 1, the continued vitality of a free press in a democracy requires first and foremost that the constitutionally guaranteed freedom of the press achieve and maintain a high level of public support. When the public is dissatisfied with the performance of the actors and organizations that compose "the press," its attitudes about press freedoms can turn negative. Can the public's affinity for those freedoms be sustained in the face of widespread public unhappiness with how particular actors and institutions in the media perform? Unless the reservoir of good will is operating at a sufficient level, support for a robust press may fall to levels below what might be considered acceptable in a democratic society dependent on a flourishing "marketplace of ideas." Given the current low levels of satisfaction with and perceived poor performance of the news media, it is particularly important to consider the state of Americans' support for press freedoms, which we do in this chapter.

A critical question now presents itself: How does one measure support for press freedoms? Even if we adhere to the premise that a robust press is critically important to democracy, there exist numerous methods by which we might test public support for its freedom. Support for the freedom of the press, we maintain, can be measured by tapping into attitudes about the freedom of the press, whether by testing approval for the actual constitutional language in question, by invoking vague references to the free press (e.g., "Do you support the First Amendment's guarantee of a free press?" "Should society tolerate broad exercises of free press?"), or by measuring support for free press rights using concrete examples of how such rights might be applied. In this chapter, then, we argue that support for freedom of the press may be conceptualized and measured both in broad abstract terms and in concrete, applied terms.

Certainly such support is in part a product of political socialization. What the individual learns early on often becomes quite stable through-

56

out his or her life. Interestingly, this political support may develop irrespective of experience and political information. Yet regardless of what theory of political socialization one subscribes to, support for the political system clearly plays an important role in the legitimacy of the system (Easton and Dennis, 1969). Indeed, the very legitimacy of a government's authority may rest on the maintenance of sufficient levels of support. And support for the system as a whole translates into support for a number of constitutional rights closely associated with that system, including the First Amendment's guarantee of freedom of the press.

EVALUATING PUBLIC SUPPORT IN AN ALTERNATIVE CONTEXT: PUBLIC OPINION AND RIGHTS OF FREE EXPRESSION

Intuitively, one expects to find a discrepancy between support for free press rights measured in the abstract, and support for the rights of the free press as they are applied in concrete circumstances. Such a discrepancy has long been a fixture in the scholarly literature analyzing comparable free expression rights. In their landmark study of civil liberties, Herbert McCloskey and Aida Brill discovered that when stated in the abstract, the liberties contained in the First Amendment are "so widely endorsed by both the general public and opinion leaders as to suggest that freedom of expression may very well be the most cherished of all American rights" (McCloskey and Brill, 1983: 48). Their results confirmed what had already been discovered in previous studies (e.g., McCloskey, 1964; Erskine, 1970). But McCloskey and Brill also concluded that freedom of expression was a "more tenuous right" than one might naturally infer from its popularity as an abstract concept alone. For example, fewer than 60 percent of the respondents in their study was willing to grant freedom of speech to people whom they considered "intolerant of the opinions of others." Only 18 percent would have permitted the American Nazi Party to use a town hall to hold a public meeting. This much is certain: Without fleshing out support for free speech rights as they are applied in more concrete circumstances, it is difficult to take statements of support for those rights very seriously.

Ironically, this apparent contradiction in the public's beliefs about freedom of expression on one hand and specific applications of that right on the other recalls a rhetorical strategy commonly employed by government officials who send out conflicting signals of their own when wrestling with the proper boundaries of civil liberties. President Harry Truman publicly extolled the virtues of liberty and civil rights in 1949 even as his own Justice Department was aggressively prosecuting Communists under the highly controversial Smith Act. In debating the merits of the Flag Protection Act of 1989 – which temporarily rendered burning of the flag a federal crime – many of the bill's supporters paid verbal tribute to the rights of "free expression and liberty" that the nation's soldiers had fought for during the previous two centuries. They even suggested that flag burning undermined those very rights.

Even the U.S. Supreme Court has indulged in a rhetorical "two-step," expressing support for free expression broadly while at the same time denying support to claimants of those same rights in certain circumstances. For example, the fundamental tenet of First Amendment law, that "government may not discriminate on the basis of the speaker's viewpoint," gave way partially in 1993 when the Court upheld a Wisconsin criminal statute that featured enhanced penalties for perpetrators acting with racially discriminatory motives.[1] And while the Supreme Court has often claimed that First Amendment rights are strongest when exercised in public places such as streets and parks, it has rarely applied that principle with much enthusiasm. During recent decades the Court has been quite deferential to the government in many so-called "public forum" cases, upholding restrictions on sound trucks,[2] the distribution of literature,[3] camping in parks as a means of protest,[4] and other so-called "time/place/manner" restrictions. Here again, little is gained from scholarly analysis of the high Court's general pronouncements about free expression under the Constitution without an understanding of how the Court views those rights when they are exercised in concrete cases.

To return to the context of public opinion: What explanations can be offered to rationalize this clear discrepancy in support for free expression rights? The numerous factors that weigh into public consideration of free expression may be understood within the framework of two different hypotheses.

The "Inconsistency Hypothesis"

Simply understood, the public assumes two fundamentally inconsistent (and perhaps hypocritical) positions in its support for free expression. Initially, citizens enthusiastically declare their fealty and allegiance to free expression in the abstract. Then, at the slightest whiff of controversy, members of the public tolerate government actions that compromise or ignore those same principles. Perhaps most citizens do not fully consider the implications of adhering to statements of abstract support when they make them. The public's inconsistent responses are thus rooted either in

---

[1] See *Wisconsin v. Mitchell*, 508 U.S. 476 (1993).
[2] *Ward v. Rock Against Racism*, 491 U.S. 781 (1989).
[3] *Heffron v. International Society for Krishna Consciousness*, 452 U.S. 640 (1981).
[4] *Clark v. Community for Creative Non-Violence*, 468 U.S. 288 (1984).

its members' own ignorance or confusion or in their oversimplified understanding of how a democracy actually works. In all likelihood, most citizens have never before linked the civil liberties heritage embodied in the Constitution in any meaningful way with less popular (and sometimes outright offensive) modes of free expression. In sum, this hypothesis holds that the public is incapable of making the connection between broad principles of freedom of press and the application of those principles to particular circumstances.

The "Qualification Hypothesis"

A less obvious possibility posits that members of the public are sophisticated consumers of civil rights and liberties, just like other governmental actors, including courts. Accordingly, members of the public who reject more libertarian applications of free speech rights in particular contexts are by no means undermining their previous declarations of abstract support for free expression; rather they are simply identifying legitimate exceptions encompassed within their own original definitions of free expression. In other words, the public's support for free expression was never absolute in the first place – when asked to respond to more general questions, members of the public answer within the context of their own cognitive framework. For example, a moderate-to-conservative citizen may genuinely express support for free expression under the First Amendment on one hand but then assume (in a logically consistent way) that the First Amendment still does not protect flag burning.[5] There may be no discrepancy at all between the two positions that a citizen holds; rather, it is simply a matter of how one chooses to define the perimeters of that liberty in the first place.

In one recent study, a group of scholars identified some of the motives that may underlie the public's refusal to apply free expression rights in more controversial circumstances (Marcus et al., 1995: 8–9). The possibilities included:

- the malice members of the public held toward certain groups simply overwhelmed their commitment to democratic values
- the public's belief that censoring "undemocratic" groups is in fact the best way to *uphold* democracy
- the public's belief that free expression is an important value but that order and stability are *more important* values

---

[5] Such a "qualification" of otherwise broad free speech rights may explain the vote of moderate Justice John Paul Stevens, for example, who dissented from the Supreme Court's speech-protective flag-burning decision in 1989 [*Texas v. Johnson*, 491 U.S. 397 (1989)], despite having assumed a more liberal stance toward free speech issues in many other cases.

Certainly each of the foregoing scenarios seriously belies the premise that an ignorant and unthinking public is reacting in a hypocritical fashion to free expression issues. In the first two scenarios, the public might never have intended to extend its support for free expression to groups so far out of the mainstream that their views may be harmful to the country. (Thus the Jewish community in Skokie, Illinois, may give diffuse support to free expression in general but then take legitimate exception to its application by Nazis' marching in their community.) And the third scenario exposes the real weakness of testing the public's support for civil liberties through abstract questions alone: The public may support numerous abstract principles without reference to the possibility that those principles sometimes clash, even in a well-functioning democracy. Accordingly, if those same general questions from the McCloskey and Brill surveys had been rewritten in such a way as to incorporate the possibility of a clash among competing values (e.g., equal protection rights versus free expression), the public might not have seemed so committed to the rights of free expression as it did when there was no such clash. But when no such hypothetical conflict is presented, support for free expression appears quite strong.

One can readily imagine any of these three scenarios at work among political elites or others possessing above-average knowledge of First Amendment law and its implications. Members of pro-choice organizations such as the National Abortion Rights League or the National Organization for Women (NOW) may genuinely believe that the Constitution does not protect the rights of groups such as Operation Rescue to make intimidating statements to people entering abortion clinics. Members of NOW may see no real contradiction in avowing their belief in freedom of speech on the one hand and their willingness to suppress anti-abortion protesters on the other; from their perspective, those groups have exceeded their right to claim constitutional protection.

Yet one might have a more difficult time accepting that the vast majority of Americans – most of whom possess little or no knowledge of First Amendment law – simply assumed a "qualified" position toward civil liberties when they answered McCloskey and Brill's inquiries about their support for free expression. But the public's definition of constitutional freedoms is not so absolute; that definition often encompasses reasonable restrictions depending upon the circumstances. In fact, the public's adherence to abstract principles of free expression (as noted in the studies cited previously) does not necessarily signal a concurrent willingness to interpret the First Amendment more broadly and liberally than even the most liberal justices on the Supreme Court have done.

Of course this dichotomy between support for an abstract freedom and support for concrete applications of that freedom is not unique to the right of free speech. As McCloskey and Brill (1983) were quick to note, a disparity has traditionally existed between the expressed attitudes toward women's rights in general and prevailing practices that limit those rights without any widespread objections. Although there is a reservoir of popular acceptance of the right of the politically disaffected to express their feelings through public assemblies, that level of support begins to drop for assemblies of Nazis and other "extreme groups" (McCloskey and Brill, 1983: 117). And while the mass public tends to endorse the free exercise of religion in general terms, that high level of support drops when, for example, the public is asked about the right of atheists to "make fun of God and religion in a public place" (McCloskey and Brill, 1983: 132). Does public support for press freedoms follow this same pattern? In the section that follows, we compare support for the abstract principle with support for the most controversial exercises of that freedom.

DIFFUSE SUPPORT FOR PRESS FREEDOMS: THE ABSTRACT VERSUS THE CONCRETE

How does the public's support for (or opposition to) the Constitution's guarantee of a free press fit within the theoretical constructs of public opinion described here? There are at least two possibilities. First, the freedom of the press may be viewed as a distinct constitutional freedom, one that enjoys its own unique tradition and historical legacy. Certainly the words of the First Amendment itself give credence to the notion that the press enjoys its own unique claim to constitutional protection: "Congress shall make no law . . . abridging the freedom of speech, *or of the press* . . ." Given this language, one might fairly view the freedom of the press as its own abstract principle worthy of public support. While we would anticipate general approval for the vague notion of a free and uncensored press, it should come as no surprise then if the level of public support were to disintegrate when applied to certain concrete circumstances.

Why would abstract support for the general right of free press be so fragile? To draw on public opinion of free expression as an analogue, the right of free press might never have been perceived in such an unbounded manner in the first place. Members of the public may be so hostile in their attitudes toward certain members of the press that this hostility simply overwhelms their commitment to those members' constitutional rights. Perhaps some members of the press are so sensational and money-driven that they tend to "corrupt" political discourse with lies to sell their publications; if so, the public might reasonably assume that censoring those individuals *protects* rather than *subverts* democracy. Finally, the public might consider other values – such as equality – to be even more important than the right of the free press. Thus, censorship of racist publications might seem like a fair price to pay in a society that aspires to guarantee fair treatment to all groups.

An alternative perspective might treat the freedom of the press as a concrete application of more broadly understood free expression rights under the First Amendment. Thus the freedom of the press does *not* exist separate from the right to free speech; rather, newspapers, magazines, and other media outlets are merely exercising their own rights of free speech under the Constitution. From this perspective, support for free press rights would be considered tantamount to support for free speech – the two are indistinguishable. Accordingly, we would expect the discrepancy between support for free press in the abstract and support for free press under more concrete circumstances to be less acute, as the abstract free press right is itself merely a concrete application of free expression as a whole.

DESCRIPTION OF THE DATA

As we suggested in Chapter 2, if support for civil liberties is high, the system is secure from the vagaries of specific events that might loosen the attachments that the masses have to the political system, thus compromising the legitimacy of the political system. We measured the abstract dimension of support for the First Amendment in several ways. In a break from past studies, respondents were first presented with the full text of the Amendment and asked, "Based on your feelings about the First Amendment, please tell me whether you agree or disagree with the following statement: The First Amendment goes too far in the rights it guarantees." Those disagreeing with this statement are those who express abstract support; those agreeing lack abstract support.[6]

We found that two-thirds of Americans either strongly (45 percent) or mildly (22 percent) disagreed with this statement, reflecting a high level of abstract support for the First Amendment as a whole. Meanwhile, only about three in ten either strongly (16 percent) or mildly (12 percent) agree that the First Amendment goes too far in the rights it guarantees. The First Amendment itself represents a cacophony of different (and in some cases unrelated) rights, but we found that support figures for the Amendment as a whole are generally positive.

---

[6] We chose to measure support from a negative perspective. A previous survey read to respondents the words of the First Amendment and then asked, if it were being voted on today, would they vote for or against it? Ninety-three percent said they would vote for it. In this study, we chose the negative perspective in order to get respondents to think about whether they feel First Amendment rights have gone too far, reducing the problem of a socially unacceptable response.

Two items gauge abstract support for the freedom of the press. The first item asks respondents if press freedoms have gone too far in guaranteeing rights, or not far enough: "Even though the U.S. Constitution guarantees freedom of the press, government has placed some restrictions on it. Overall, do you think the press in America has too much freedom to do what it wants, too little freedom to do what it wants, or is the amount of freedom the press has about right?"

We interpreted the "too little" and "about right" responses to this item to measure positive abstract support for the current state of the First Amendment's freedom of the press. Generally positive feelings about press rights would lead individuals to say the rights are appropriate, or should be applied to an even greater degree. By contrast, those who feel that press rights are overextended would exhibit lower levels of abstract support. This same item was also included on a survey conducted by CSRA in July 1997, offering tracking data on possible short-term changes in abstract support for constitutionally guaranteed press freedoms.

Figure 4.1 depicts abstract support for press rights of the First Amendment by asking whether the press has "too much," "too little," or "about the right amount of" freedom. In March 1999, less than a majority felt that the press had either the right amount of freedom (37 percent) or too little freedom (7 percent). Additionally, there is a large and significant drop over the twenty-month period in those feeling that the press has either too little or about the right amount of freedom. In July 1997, 59 percent felt that way, compared with only 44 percent who expressed abstract support in the 1999 survey. Why the drop? In all likelihood, the Clinton-Lewinsky story galvanized public criticism and general hostility toward the press's performance, including its obsession with the story. That hypothesis was confirmed in the spring of 2000 – more than a year after the president's impeachment trial – when support for free press rights was already showing signs of climbing back up. Specifically, 48

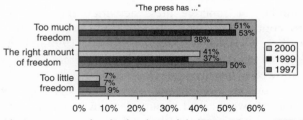

Figure 4.1. Abstract support for the freedom of the press. (Source: CSRA University of Connecticut Surveys, 1997, 1999, and 2000.)

percent felt the press had too little or the right amount of freedom in our April 2000 survey.

We used one additional item to measure support for press freedom in the abstract. The item directly asks respondents about their opinion regarding the freedom of the press to provide news. This time, however, respondents were *not* asked whether there is currently too much or too little freedom. Instead, respondents were asked only to agree or disagree with the following statement: "News organizations should be allowed to report or publicize what they think is appropriate to report."

A clear majority (66 percent) agreed with this statement. The differentiation respondents made between press freedoms and other freedoms (such as freedom of speech) is readily apparent – in a related question in our study focusing on free expression, a full 89 percent of respondents were willing to lend support for free speech rights to the public, "whatever their views might be." Despite these unfavorable comparisons with free expression, the level of measured support for press freedoms in this item is still relatively high as compared with the previous item. And perhaps even more significantly, this support score is comparable to support scores for the First Amendment as a whole, belying the interpretation that press freedoms are mere stepchild rights within that amendment.

As noted previously, while support for broad systemic constructs (such as the First Amendment) has achieved high levels from the American public, that support often drops precipitously once concrete examples are offered. Reactions to these specific examples form the basis for measures of support at the concrete level. In our study, we measured Americans' concrete support for press rights by administering a set of questions that asked whether or not media organizations should enjoy discretion in certain specific circumstances. Specifically, we asked whether respondents "strongly agree," "mildly agree," "mildly disagree," or "strongly disagree" that media organizations should be allowed to exercise their free press rights in ten specific situations.

Table 4.1 depicts responses to the ten concrete support items related to freedom of the press. As a whole, Americans in 1999 were supportive of a number of concrete press activities and resist government attempts to control the Fourth Estate. Still, some hemorrhaging of support for these press rights between 1997 and 1999 is evident. Of the eight items asked in both 1997 and 1999, all but item 3 ("Should broadcasters be allowed to televise courtroom trials?") showed a decrease in support by the public. The discrepancy on item 3 is easily explainable: When respondents were asked about televising trials in 1997, the O. J. Simpson trial and its aftermath (the civil trial, the battle for custody of Simpson's children, etc.) were still fresh in the public mind. Once the ver-

use in SLC 225

Table 4.1. Concrete Support for the Freedom of the Press

	% Specific Support	
	1997	1999
"Newspapers should be allowed to publish freely without government approval of a story"	80	65
"Newspapers should be allowed to keep a news source confidential"	85	79
"Broadcasters should be allowed to televise courtroom trials"	51	67
"Newspapers should be allowed to endorse or criticize political candidates"	69	63
"The news media should be allowed to report government secrets that have come to journalists' attention"	61	48
"Television networks should be allowed to project winners of an election while people are still voting"	31	29
"High school students should be allowed to report controversial issues in their student newspapers without school approval"	45	37
"Journalists should be allowed to use hidden cameras in their reporting"	31	27
"Broadcasters should be allowed to televise the proceedings of the U.S. Supreme Court"	–	73
"Journalists should be allowed to investigate the private lives of public figures"	–	38

Note: The percentages in each column represent the percent that "strongly agrees" or "mildly agrees" that the press should be afforded the specific right mentioned.
Source: CSRA University of Connecticut Survey, 1997 and 1999.

dicts in Simpson's civil trial were announced in January 1998, the public could once again give the matter more fair and reasoned consideration. For a period of more than three years, the media had overreported and sensationalized every single detail of the Simpson affair, crowding out other news in the process. Although the O. J. Simpson case may never recede completely from the public's view, it now takes its position as one of a handful of public opinion–altering events of the late 1990s. By contrast, the 2000 presidential election continued to focus attention on the Clinton-Lewinsky episode in 1999, eroding support for the freedom of the press in the abstract and, to a lesser extent, more concrete freedoms. (Item 10, an obvious reference to the Clinton-Lewinsky matter in the public's mind, garnered only 38 percent support.)

Almost eight in ten agreed that journalists should be allowed to keep a news source confidential. Coverage of legal events also obtains heavy public support; 67 percent agreed that broadcasters should be allowed to televise courtroom trials, and more than seven in ten Americans favor televising the proceedings of the U.S. Supreme Court. More than six in ten favor newspapers' endorsing or criticizing political candidates. Finally, Americans are twice as likely to agree than to disagree that newspapers should be allowed to publish freely without governmental approval. This final statistic represents a dip from the 1997 survey, when an overwhelming 80 percent supported press rights in this context. Once again, the Clinton-Lewinsky affair appears to have had a significant impact on the public's trust of news organizations. More significantly, these concrete examples may represent instances in which other values (right to a fair trial, etc.) are deemed *more important* to the public than the freedom of the press standing alone, contributing to the evidence in support of the "qualification hypothesis." Otherwise, it would be hard to explain why any concrete items would garner higher levels of support than the abstract notion of freedom of the press.

There are also a number of concrete press activities that set off red flags among the public, many of which are protective of other values at issue in those activities. Few Americans support networks' projecting winners of an election while people are still voting (29 percent), a case where free press values compete with values of fairness in voting. Still fewer support the use of hidden cameras in journalists' reporting (27 percent), a circumstance in which free press values compete with notions of privacy, honesty, and fair play. Only 37 percent believe that high school students should be allowed to report controversial issues in their newspapers without school approval, a nod to the importance that school discipline holds in the public's mind. And less than half (48 percent) favor the news media's reporting government secrets that have come to their attention. Finally, fewer than four in ten agree that journalists should be allowed to investigate the private lives of public figures.

In sum, we find mixed results: Some concrete items show relatively high levels of support for press rights, while other items attract far lower levels of support. Half of the ten examples garnered concrete support levels above 50 percent among the general public. All this points to the "qualification hypothesis" at work: The public support of freedom of the press more or less depends upon what other freedoms are placed in conflict with it. Sometimes concrete items invoke references to other values in addition to the free press, and they receive support levels higher than abstract support levels for freedom of the press alone. In other instances the more classic trailing off of support for concrete items is quite evident.

In the data analysis section that follows, we do the following: (1) examine the determinants of support for the First Amendment as a whole, and the freedom of the press in particular; (2) examine the determinants of concrete support for the freedom of the press; and (3) evaluate the relationship between the two dimensions – abstract and concrete – of support.

ANALYSIS OF THE DATA AND ITS DETERMINANTS

Determinants of Abstract Support for the First Amendment

In measuring abstract support for the First Amendment, we find a number of demographic groups and other population segments exhibiting varying levels of abstract support. Table 4.2 depicts some of these differences. Income and education clearly bear a strong relationship to abstract support for the First Amendment; as income and education levels increase, so does abstract support in both cases. This is not surprising given that broader, more abstract, positive feelings about the political system are likely to be influenced by the economic well-being and security enjoyed by an individual. The influence of education may also build up an appreciation for political tolerance of civil liberties. Economic resources tend to influence the quality of life and happiness of an individual, and so those with greater family incomes (who therefore benefit from greater economic resources) are more likely to maintain more positive feelings about the political system in general. This clearly is the case with respect to generalized abstract support for the First Amendment. More than eight in ten Americans with family incomes over $75,000 express abstract support for the First Amendment, while fewer than six in ten with family incomes under $30,000 express abstract support for those constitutional guarantees.

The lower level of abstract support among those in the oldest age group is also interesting. It tends to support Easton's notion that the reservoir of good feelings is developed at a young age and tends to erode as one gets older. While we detect only modest changes in abstract support from the youngest age group to the forty-five to sixty-one cohort, abstract support drops off significantly at or near the age of retirement.

An individual's level of knowledge about First Amendment issues as well as his or her overall level of engagement and involvement in politics also appears to contribute to abstract support levels, with the more knowledgeable and more engaged exhibiting higher support. Indeed, it appears that knowledge and understanding of First Amendment issues breed greater appreciation for the abstract right of freedom of the press. Likewise, engagement and involvement in political processes also lead to a greater appreciation of that right.

Table 4.2. Variations in General Abstract Support for the First Amendment by Demographic Groups

	% Abstract Support
Total	67
Education:	
High school or less	55
Some college	73
College	82
Age:	
18–29	73
30–44	68
45–61	70
62+	57
Income:	
Under 30 K	59
30–50 K	67
50–75 K	78
75 K+	84
Ideology:	
Liberal	73
Moderate	74
Conservative	64
Knowledge of First Amendment:	
Low	62
Moderate	70
High	73
Political involvement:	
Low	60
Moderate	70
High	78

Note: The percentages in this table represent the percent who disagree that the First Amendment goes too far in protecting freedoms.

Source: CSRA University of Connecticut Survey, 1997.

Determinants of Abstract Support for the Freedom of the Press

What explains the relatively low level of abstract support for press rights (as compared with support for the First Amendment as a whole)? One answer lies in the public's own assessment of the press's performance during recent years – particularly in evaluations of media coverage of the Clinton-Lewinsky story. As we noted in Chapter 1, a late 1998 survey of the American public found that most Americans had heard enough about President Clinton's personal affairs.[7] Nearly seven in ten (69 percent) said the media went too far in disclosing the details of the president's private life. Meanwhile, the difference between the public and the press was never before so pronounced, as 56 percent of news directors thought the media went as far as was right when disclosing the details of President Clinton's private life. Overall these surveys found that the public's assessment of the news media's performance in covering this story was very low, with a substantial majority giving the media failing grades for coverage.

Little changed in public perceptions of the press and its handling of this story in subsequent months. By March 1999, 68 percent of Americans felt the press had gone too far in reporting on Clinton's personal life.[8] Clearly the public's attitudes about coverage of the Clinton-Lewinsky story are quite critical. Much of the public believed the news media excessively covered this story at the expense of other important news. The public felt that the news media sensationalized the story by dwelling on the sexual aspects of what occurred, and the public had serious questions about the motivations of the press in providing so much coverage to this story, perhaps feeling that coverage was largely influenced by the desire to sell papers and magazines and increase audiences rather than to get the facts of the events that occurred.

It is quite possible, then, that the media as a whole have lost credibility as a result of their coverage of the Clinton-Lewinsky story, and that this loss has in turn influenced public opinion about press freedoms in general. Subsequently, when Americans are asked about their generalized support for a free press, the object on which they form an opinion – the media – contributes to their response. Thus the specific coverage of Clinton-Lewinsky, negatively viewed by the American public, appears to have had the effect of partially draining positive affection people hold for a free press. Accordingly, we explore the differential levels of broad support for press freedoms between various segments of the population and evaluate the relative strength various factors (e.g., education level, income, political orientations) may have in contributing to the higher levels of abstract support for free expression.

---

[7] See Kenneth Dautrich et al., "The Disconnect Between News Directors and the Public: Explaining Why Americans Are Cynical About the News." Study conducted by CSRA, May 1999.

[8] Ken Dautrich and Thomas Hartley, "The Effects of News Coverage of the Clinton/Lewinsky Story on Public Attitudes of the News Media." Paper presented at the annual meeting of the American Association for Public Opinion Research, May 1999.

Table 4.3. Variations in Abstract Support for the
Freedom of the Press by Demographic Groups

	% Abstract Support
Total	44
Education:	
High school or less	39
Some college	44
College	58
Age:	
18–29	42
30–45	43
45–61	50
62+	40
Income:	
Under 30K	39
30–50K	41
50–75K	54
75K+	57
Ideology:	
Liberal	52
Moderate	46
Conservative	41
Knowledge of First Amendment:	
Low	34
Medium–low	36
Medium–high	54
High	60
Political involvement:	
Low	42
Moderate	44
High	50

Note: The percentages in this table represent the percent that
thinks the press in the United States has "too little freedom to
do what it wants" or thinks the amount of freedom the press
has is "about right."
Source: CSRA University of Connecticut Survey, 1999.

On the first item of abstract support for freedom of the press – which
measures whether the public believes the freedom of the press goes "too
far" – income and education again bear an especially strong relationship
to levels of public support (see Table 4.3). However, unlike with measures of support for the First Amendment in general, bombardments of

Clinton-Lewinsky coverage created a far greater range of support scores. Education and income do not simply build an appreciation for the freedom of the press; in the final analysis, those variables actually make a difference between minority and majority support for this fundamental right. More than six in ten Americans who have either not been educated beyond high school or who earn less than $30,000 per year believe the freedom of press has gone too far. As with the First Amendment support scores, we detect an erosion of support for the freedom of the press among those sixty-two years or older. And general knowledge of constitutional rights pays off in support for individual freedoms such as the freedom of the press, as a majority of those with medium-to-high or high knowledge of the First Amendment expresses support for the freedom of the press.

Without hinting at any concrete context or circumstance, the second item of abstract support for press freedoms asks specifically about the exercise of discretion by news organizations to publish or report what they think is appropriate. As with item 1, income, education, and general knowledge of the First Amendment all influence support for this more abstract press right of news organizations. What seems more remarkable is the high level of support for this right that exists across the board. Of all the different demographic groups listed in Table 4.4, only those from the lowest income group offered less than 60 percent support for this general right. Meanwhile, all groups supported the right by a clear majority, and *over three-quarters* of two groups (those who make between $50,000 and $75,000 and those with high knowledge of the First Amendment) supported the right as well.

Clearly, even if the Clinton-Lewinsky scandal had a negative impact on public support for the freedom of the press in the abstract, a reservoir of positive feelings remains for the right of news organizations to publish freely. This discrepancy may be explained in at least two ways. First, the public may be driven by its sense of whether the press is acting according to its own belief systems about what is appropriate. If the public believes news organizations are abandoning all sense of "appropriateness" to sell newspapers, then it may believe that the current state of press freedoms goes beyond the right addressed in item 2. Second, the public appears to be more enthusiastic about the news product itself (as symbolized by the right to publish freely) than it is about the overall conduct of the media (as measured by the state of the freedom of the press in general). Dautrich and Hartley (1999) discovered this discrepancy at work in studying how voters graded the media. The specific criticisms that voters leveled at the news media related not as much to the news product provided but to how the news media conducted themselves in influencing the electoral process. The same may hold true in this

Table 4.4. Variations in Abstract Support for News
Organizations to "Publish or Report What They
Think Is Appropriate" by Demographic Groups

	% Abstract Support
Total	66
Education:	
High school or less	62
Some college	66
College	73
Age:	
18–29	68
30–44	68
45–61	62
62+	64
Income:	
Under 30 K	58
30–50 K	65
50–75 K	77
75 K+	73
Ideology:	
Liberal	73
Moderate	70
Conservative	62
Knowledge of First Amendment	
Low	60
Medium–low	64
Medium–high	66
High	78
Political involvement:	
Low	64
Moderate	66
High	69

Note: The percentages in this table represent the percent who
agree that "news organizations should be allowed to report or
publish" what they think is appropriate.
Source: CSRA University of Connecticut Survey, 1999.

context, as the public in effect uses general freedom of the press questions as its opportunity to criticize media conduct in general.

Thus in the final analysis, the reservoir of good will toward the press
appears strong, at least from a review of support measuring the abstract
dimension. Although Americans have been deeply frustrated by events

Table 4.5. Specific Support for Free Press Index

Score: 0	1%
1	4
2	5
3	9
4	12
5	17
6	19
7	14
8	10
9	7
10	2
	100%

Source: CSRA University of Connecticut Survey, 1999.

of the past few years, they are still highly skeptical of any attempts to curtail news organizations' discretion. We now turn to an examination of support for press rights measured from the concrete dimension.

Evaluating the Relationship Between Concrete and Abstract Support for Press Freedoms

What about the degree to which abstract and concrete support are consistent or inconsistent? Past research found that abstract and concrete support are often inconsistent – that while Americans typically exhibit high abstract support levels for constitutional rights, there is often a steep drop-off when it comes to concrete manifestations of these freedoms. In this section we address the extent of the relationship between the abstract concept of free press and the concrete situations where that First Amendment freedom is put to the test.

To examine this relationship, we use the most general measure of abstract support for the free press – that is, the item that asked Americans if they agree or disagree that "News organizations should be allowed to report what they think is appropriate to report." To measure concrete press support, we created an index that gave one point to each respondent for each time he or she agreed with one of the ten items presented in Table 4.1. Table 4.5 provides the distributions for the index. Our study found a statistically significant relationship between the abstract press and concrete press measures (.30). While statistically significant, however, the substantive correlation is a modest one. Thus there is, in fact, a fair amount of slippage between the abstract support for freedom of the press and the extent to which Americans feel that the freedom of the press should be extended under extenuating circumstances.

The relatively weak relationship between the press measures is likely a function of the lower relative levels of abstract support for free press, compared with other freedoms. It may also signal support for the "qualification hypothesis," proof that the public adopts a sophisticated view of constitutional freedoms such as freedom of the press, weighing that freedom against competing values. As described earlier, lower levels of abstract support for free press may also be the result of Americans' experience with the press's coverage of the Clinton-Lewinsky story. The reservoir of good will (measured at the abstract level) for the freedom of the press may have dipped as a result of popular dissatisfaction with the news media coverage of these events. A high correlation between the press measures, then, may be a reflection of drained levels of abstract support from recent bombarding events.

CONCLUSION

When discussed in the abstract, press freedoms do not normally receive the same high levels of popular support that many other constitutional freedoms garner. Rights of free expression, for example, usually receive overwhelming approval from the masses. Nevertheless, the freedom of the press still has a lot going for it. Despite considerable ill will directed at the press in recent years, the public remains highly resistant to any attempt to curtail newsgathering freedoms or the discretion to publish. Unlike with other civil liberties, Americans maintain an especially thoughtful approach to press freedoms: While they often dislike individual members of the press and show a distaste for their "sensationalistic" coverage of recent events, they are generally unwilling to abandon the freedoms that lie at the core of the "liberty of the press." Indeed, in many cases, support for concrete press freedoms has actually risen.

Perhaps the public deserves credit for adopting such a highly sophisticated and rational approach to the freedom of the press. The reservoir of good will that exists toward press freedoms as a whole – bombarded as that reservoir has been in recent years – still has enough in reserve to fend off any attempt to convert distrust of the press into a curtailment of press rights. In fact, support remains stronger than ever for certain press freedoms. Such a reservoir may not be maintained indefinitely – at some point this good will may dry up if the press overplays its hand in the years to come. But for now, the press remains in the public's good graces, secure in the assumption that the public supports the function that it purports to perform in a political democracy.

5

Support for Press Freedoms Across Media: Comparing Print, Electronic, and the "New Media"

When William Blackstone penned his now-classic *Commentaries on the Laws of England* in 1769, he spoke of the "liberty of press" as being "essential to the nature of a free state." Among Blackstone's contemporaries, there was probably little confusion about the nature of the "press" to which he was referring. Ever since the advent of printing presses several centuries earlier, so-called "printers" had assumed their place in western Europe and elsewhere as disseminators of information. When referring to the "press," Blackstone was speaking primarily (if not entirely) about those producers and distributors of printed materials: newspapers, pamphlets, and other written instruments that had become dominant elements of western European culture by the mid–eighteenth century. Notably, this description of the press as comprising primarily written and printed materials had not changed substantially by the time the First Amendment was ratified in 1791, as newspapers and pamphlets remained the most significant modes of mass communication in the world of the Framers (de Sola Pool, 1983:2). Nor would the character of the press change to any substantial degree during the century that followed.

It was not until the growth of radio and television as news and entertainment sources in the early and middle parts of the twentieth century that the term "press" came to encompass far more than printed materials. Radio and television reporters would soon be considered members of the press as well. Given this suddenly expanding definition of "press," either the scope and protection afforded by the "freedom of the press" would have to expand accordingly, or the legal system would have to account for a heretofore unprecedented category of "unprotected media."

In particular, radio assumed its own unique place in American culture. The radio became a focus of family entertainment; realizing radio's inherent power, President Franklin Delano Roosevelt used his famous "fireside chats" on the air to keep American citizens abreast of various economic and wartime developments. Then, beginning in the 1950s, television transformed the communications landscape in even more fundamental ways. Today the average American family is tuned into the TV for more than a third of its waking hours, and television has become the single most important source of news, information, and entertainment for most citizens. More recently, the Internet has exploded onto the scene to serve as yet another source of information for the average citizen. Does the American public, which has come to rely so heavily on these new media sources, believe they should be accorded the same degree of protection as more traditional forms of press, such as newspapers and periodicals? Why or why not? In this chapter we investigate the extent to which both the legal system and the public in fact treat alternative types of media quite differently, and we place this differential treatment in the context of Americans' support for the freedom of the press as a whole.

RADIO, TELEVISION, AND THE RISE OF ALTERNATIVE FORMS OF MEDIA

As already noted, the news industry has undergone dramatic changes during the past half century. Consider the vast expansion of the newspaper industry alone. At the beginning of World War II there were just three competing national news services: the Associated Press, United Press International, and the International News Service (Powe, 1991: 208). Although a handful of national newspapers such as the *New York Times* could afford to support national correspondents in Washington, D.C., and elsewhere, most newspapers relied on these services (primarily the Associated Press and United Press International) for news outside their respective geographical areas. Every reporter on a member newspaper provided news to all other news service members. In return, the news services' capacity to provide local news from all over North America was unparalleled.

Although radio and television emerged as alternative media during the twentieth century, newspapers remained the dominant news source at least up until the 1960s, in part because broadcasters only rarely had the opportunity to capitalize on their technological advantages. For example, the U.S. military strictly limited the ability of television reporters to cover the Korean War directly from the battlefield. The amount of time allotted by networks to news broadcasts on television was also quite limited. By contrast, newspapers and magazines were able to cover major news events with considerably more comprehension and depth than any of these other competing media sources. Thus for a long time, "freedom of the press" was considered primarily a rallying cry for newspaper and magazine reporters to discover and report on facts and information, including (but not limited to) controversial criminal trials, corrupt government practices, and other sources of official embarrassment. During the early 1960s it was the *New York Times* and other national news organizations that had to defend themselves in court against lawsuits brought by southern officials digging in against the advances of the civil rights movement. And as late as 1971, when the Pentagon Papers case became the latest cause célèbre for the freedom of the press, it was two competing dailies, the *New York Times* and the *Washington* Post, that fought the Nixon administration all the way up to the U.S. Supreme Court.

What about other forms of news media? While radio had been around longer, it was the medium of television that would come to rival and even surpass printed materials as a daily news source. Television's heavy influence over ordinary citizens' views of American politics and politicians dates back at least to 1960, when the nationally televised presidential debates between Richard Nixon and John F. Kennedy were credited with assisting Kennedy's victory over Nixon later that fall (Lang and Lang, 1968). Yet it was the events surrounding the civil rights movement and the Vietnam War that gave citizens a real taste of what this new medium could achieve. From coverage of those two historical crises, television established its worth as a unique means of conveying certain news and information. According to a recent Roper Center survey, local television news now dwarfs most other news sources in its use and popularity, with 80 percent of Americans indicating that they watch these local news broadcasts at least several times per week.[1]

In his highly influential work *Understanding Media* (1967), Marshall McLuhan argued that media technology itself could transform lives to an even greater extent than the substance of the messages that were actually being transmitted. Whereas radio was considered a "hot" medium that required listeners to convert its messages from verbal to mental imagery, television was the "cool medium" that pulled the viewer in. When viewed on a television screen, those same messages and information provided a largely passive experience for the audience. Thus McLuhan coined the phrase "The medium is the message." Television figuratively pulled the public into it, shaping every aspect of the news and information for an otherwise inactive public. Those who criticized civil rights protesters as "troublemakers" and "dissidents" found it

---

[1] In fact, 54 percent of the public indicated they watched local television news *every day*. See "Americans' Views of the News: What They Like, What They Don't Like, and What Sources They Use." Study Sponsored by the Freedom Forum, conducted by the Roper Center for Public Opinion Research, University of Connecticut, February 1997, p. 8.

especially difficult to reconcile those preconceived notions with the images of official violence that poured forth nightly from the evening news. And unlike past wars that often proved to be propaganda boons for the government, the Vietnam conflict could not be glorified so easily, as images of an unsuccessful war came across so vividly to viewers on the small screen.

Of course McLuhan was writing two decades before the explosion of talk radio and cable television stations, and nearly thirty years before the vast expansion of the Internet. Nevertheless, he envisioned that television would foster an electronic world community, what he termed "a global village." For all his foresight and vision, McLuhan could not have anticipated the rise of the Internet. Television was structurally limited to transmitting the messages of those with the resources to purchase air time, and its audience was inherently passive, with little or no interactive capacity. In short, it was a global village where only a few voices would be routinely heard. By contrast, the technological media revolution of the past twenty years has altered the communications landscape considerably, expanding the channels of communication between the press and the public (Davis and Owen, 1998). The definition of "press" would similarly be forced to expand, or various new forms of media would be left bereft of important constitutional protections. A number of new controversies soon arose over whether the First Amendment should apply equally to all forms of media. The many disparate elements of the controversial "new media" include the following:

Talk Radio

A decade after Watergate, the American political system found itself polarized. A political tug of war was waged at various levels between the ardent, Reagan-led political conservatives who controlled the executive branch throughout the 1980s and the Democrats who controlled the House of Representatives during that same period, as epitomized by the old liberal warrior Speaker Thomas P. "Tip" O'Neill (D-Mass.). In the late 1980s, various radio stations searching for ways to enhance their revenue tapped into an ever-growing number of listeners frustrated with the gridlock in Washington. In fact, talk radio exploded just as Americans' frustration with government and politics was reaching record levels. The radio audience as a whole was also expanding during this period. Greater numbers of people began working within their homes, where radios kept them company. Meanwhile, the proliferation of mobile phones gave commuters trapped in traffic a ready outlet to participate in political discussions. Eventually, the election of Bill Clinton in 1992 – perhaps the most polarizing national leader since Richard Nixon – fueled the ire of conservative radio listeners who frequented talk shows hosted by Rush Limbaugh, G. Gordon Liddy, and Oliver North, among other conservatives. Talk radio has thus managed to amass its own mass audience today, with 25 percent of the public admitting that they listen to talk radio shows at least weekly.[2] Clearly, radio as a medium has catapulted itself back into a position of increased importance in the political dialogue (Hoftsetter et al., 1994). Talk show programming is now featured on some radio stations, twenty-four hours per day, in nearly every major metropolitan area in the United States.

Cable Television Stations

In 1970, most television sets in America were equipped to carry up to thirteen VHF channels, as well as a handful of UHF channels. The growth of cable television expanded the number and variety of television channels that reached the masses. Local-access channels make television airtime available to members of the public at a nominal fee, opening up the medium of television to groups that would otherwise have been compelled to look elsewhere. Nationally, cable television also spelled the beginning of the end of television dominance by the three major television networks: ABC, CBS, and NBC. As cable networks proliferated, they were able to offer reduced rates to subscribers and increased opportunities to watch television shows that would have been unable to break into the network schedule. The Home Box Office network (HBO) was one of the first to forgo commercials entirely, and a host of others quickly followed. CNN and Fox each developed their own twenty-four-hour-per-day news channels, allowing the public to view events such as the Persian Gulf War in "real time." Today, fully 76 percent of the American public subscribes to some form of cable TV.[3] And even the most basic cable package features a minimum of forty channels for its customers; meanwhile, those with satellite dishes can access virtually thousands of channels at any time of the day.

The Internet

The emergence of the Internet as a universal broadcast medium during the 1990s may have been the most profound development in mass communications since the advent of the printing press. Suddenly, the definition of "press" expanded to include millions of desktop publishers – literally anyone with a computer and a modem can disseminate his or opinions or other information to members of the public through chat groups, World Wide Web pages, or other Internet outlets.

---

[2] Ibid.   [3] Ibid.

The interactive nature of this new medium has contributed directly to its significance. As with talk radio, the public can now communicate directly with members of the press and the public as a whole on an immediate basis, commenting on the news or information provided to them. And as with other forms of "new" media, there is clearly a mass audience for the Internet: Half of all Americans today enjoy some form of access to the medium, and 24 percent report using the Internet to get news and information.

Unlike with "interactive radio," however, no credentials (whether formal or informal) are required from those who either distribute the news and information at its initial stages on the Internet or who monitor the discussions that take place there. Thus on the Internet, the terms "public" and "press" seem almost interchangeable. Nearly every mainstream news organization has tried to tap into this new phenomenon by producing its own heavily visited Web site. This last development has also had direct implications on the quality of news. News organizations publishing on the Internet are now unfettered by deadlines; accordingly, reporters work without the benefit of a fixed window of time to check sources and verify facts. An overall dilution of news standards – inevitable given the vast proliferation of news and information distributors on the Internet – has become a vexing problem for more established news organizations competing in this new, unregulated form of media.

Nontraditional Uses of More Conventional Media Forms

Along with technologically advanced media forms, individuals have turned to more traditional devices for conveying information, using them in innovative new ways. Directors of full-length motion pictures have often been accused of attempting to further their own political agendas, and now so-called "docudramas" routinely straddle the line between documentaries and works of fiction. Thus, for example, Oliver Stone's "historical" accounts of the Kennedy assassination and Richard Nixon's presidency mixed a selection of facts with artistic license to achieve box office success. Billboards, traditionally the exclusive province of commercial advertisers, now commonly feature political ideas and advertisements promoting candidates and interest groups. John Lennon used his songs to argue for world peace; more recently, rappers and other controversial recording artists have tried to convey not-so-subtle political and social messages through their own recordings. When the term "press" is so broadly defined, it becomes difficult to exclude various forms of art – music, dance, sculpture, or even paintings – that convey some sentiments of their creators, whether political or otherwise. All of these media forms are now commonly used to transmit news, information, and opinions to the public.

The "freedom of the press" to which Blackstone referred – later incorporated into the First Amendment – could not have encompassed much more than the freedom of newspaper publishers, pamphleteers, and others with access to printing presses to distribute materials without fear of restraint. Two centuries later, the "press" has become a multi-layered patchwork of print reporters, television networks, radio talk show hosts, artists, and Internet publishers. Does the constitutionally guaranteed freedom of the press afford each of these media forms equal levels of protection? Should all such media enjoy the same degree of discretion to publish information? In the remaining sections of this chapter we contrast the legal system's approach to this problem with public sentiments on the subject. If there is public reluctance to apply principles of the free press even-handedly to disparate media forms, that reluctance could well threaten the integrity of those same principles. On the other hand, such reluctance might also signify a reasoned public approach to maintaining the continuing success of this ever-more-crowded "marketplace of ideas."

THE HIGH COURT'S APPROACH TO REGULATING THE NEW MEDIA

In 1941, Professor Zechariah Chafee of the Harvard Law School identified what would become a dominant issue in First Amendment jurisprudence during the remaining part of the century: whether or not affirmative governmental action to facilitate the freedom of expression could be justified under any circumstance (Chafee, 1941). Taken to its extreme, this type of regulatory action could effectively trample the right of news organizations to publish information at their own discretion. In the case of electronic broadcasters' enjoying access to scarce radio and television frequencies, such regulation would essentially allow the government to decide who may enjoy the right to broadcast in the first place. Under what circumstances, if any, might such intervention be justified?

In theory, those who publish newspapers, journals, and pamphlets are not relying on scarce channels of communication. Still, one could argue that given their historic role as facilitators of public debate (especially in the context of elections), newspapers should at least be subject to regulations that require them to provide access to underfunded candidates or other speakers. Where tried, however, such legislative efforts have run up against constitutional barriers. In a series of decisions in the 1970s, the Supreme Court consistently upheld the editorial rights of newspapers over competing statutory rights of access for victims of political attack.[4] As noted Constitutional Scholar Laurence Tribe has explained, entrusting government with the power to ensure media access entails at least three dangers: (1) the danger of deterring those items of coverage that will trigger duties of affording access at the media's expense; (2) the danger of inviting manipulation of the media by whichever bureaucrats are entrusted to assure access; and (3) the danger of escalating from access regulation to much more dubious exercises of governmental control (Tribe, 1988: 1002). In the context of government regulation of printed materials, those risks have carried considerable weight with the U.S. Supreme Court.

Ironically, while First Amendment immunity reigns supreme in the realm of print media, it has been diminished somewhat when applied to modern media forms such as television and radio broadcasting. In these less traditional contexts, the Supreme Court has consistently upheld restrictive broadcasting requirements under the theory that government must be able to guard against undue interference with scarce frequencies. The Court's fear that access to a limited number of working radio and television channels might be monopolized by just a few carriers with limited political and social perspectives has encouraged it to forge a constitutional line between the protection of print and broadcast news sources. Thus as early as 1943, the Supreme Court held that the Federal Communication Commission (FCC) could distribute radio licenses based on their potential "service to the community."[5] The Court similarly gave its approval to regulations requiring that broadcasters provide fair coverage of opposing viewpoints on controversial public issues.[6] And in 1978, the Court refused to limit the FCC's power to regulate "indecent" language, even though that same offending speech clearly would have been protected had it been published in a newspaper or some other printed medium.[7] Outwardly, the Court has paid lip service to the notion that broadcasters perform an important editorial function for the public; but in practice, the Court has consistently bent to arguments invoking the dilemma of "technological scarcity." The level of "invasiveness" of these broadcast media has also figured somewhat into the Court's reasoning: Television and radio are considered far more intrusive than newspapers, as offending material may enter the home in sight or sound without any real warning to consumers.

---

[4] See *Miami Herald Publishing Co. v. Tornillo*, 418 U.S. 241 (1974); *Wooley v. Maynard*, 430 U.S. 705 (1977).
[5] *National Broadcasting Co. v. United States*, 319 U.S. 190 (1943).
[6] See *Red Lion Broadcasting Co. v. F.C.C.*, 395 U.S. 367 (1969).
[7] *FCC v. Pacifica Foundation*, 438 U.S. 726 (1978).

Thus the principle that radio and television broadcasters enjoy some-what more limited constitutional protection than their brethren in the print media has been a jurisprudential fixture for decades. Somewhat less clear is the status enjoyed by newer media forms that are not plagued by the problem of "technological scarcity." Cable television outlets provide significantly greater broadcast access to members of the public than do network television stations. The Internet affords all levels of independent publishers unprecedented access to the public to dissemi-nate information. To date, the courts have rejected all attempts to regu-late these new media forms. Thus content and "indecency" regulations of cable television have consistently failed to withstand constitutional scrutiny.[8] And in *Reno v. ACLU*,[9] the Supreme Court invalidated the Communications Decency Act of 1996, which included two provisions designed to protect minors from "indecent" and "patently offensive" communications on the Internet. In its opinion, the Court rejected the idea that the Internet was a "scarce" expressive commodity; rather, "it provides relatively unlimited, low-cost capacity for communications of all kinds."

At the time this book went to press, the constitutionality of a newly modified 1998 federal law, the On-Line Child Protection Act, was being challenged in the U.S. Supreme Court.[10] Whether this or any other reg-ulation of the Internet will ever be upheld, however, remains to be seen. The Supreme Court recognized in *Reno v. ACLU* that the Internet was not as "invasive" as radio or television; communications over the Inter-net do not invade an individual's home or appear on one's computer screen any more than a newspaper invades a home and opens up to a particular page. But new Internet technology may eventually take on invasive characteristics, rendering this pillar of the Court's reasoning ever more strained. And the proliferation of cable channels could make tele-vision seem more and more like the Internet in this regard, freeing tele-vision broadcasters from the well-established constitutional strictures that apply to their colleagues in the "free television" industry.

Clearly the technological revolution of the late twentieth century has made it increasingly difficult for courts to rely on rules that have applied to all media in the past. Press technology lurches forward by the day, if not the hour. To their credit, courts have endeavored to apply First Amendment rules based on concerns of "access," "invasiveness," and the impact that regulation of media forms may have on the overall free

---

[8] See, for example, *Home Box Office, Inc. v. FCC*, 567 F.2d 9 (D.C. Cir. 1977); *Wilkinson v. Jones*, 800 F.2d 989 (10th Cir. 1986).

[9] 521 U.S. 844 (1997).

[10] See *Ashcroft v. ACLU*, Case No. 00–1293 (U.S. Sup. Ct.) (*cert.* granted, May 21, 2001).

exchange of ideas. For the Supreme Court, the interest in encouraging freedom of expression in a democratic society seemingly outweighs any theoretical but unproven benefit of censorship. Yet is the public driven by similar concerns? A comprehensive look at the public's approach to this vexing problem provides some clear indication that the public is also willing to differentiate among contrasting types of media in the level of protection they are to receive. How they do so may have implications on the state of the freedom of the press more generally.

SURVEYING THE PUBLIC ON THE APPLICATION OF PRESS FREEDOMS TO CONTRASTING MEDIA FORMS

Examining the effects of "medium type" on support for free press rights requires that we measure public willingness to extend those rights across various media. Our strategy of measuring the limits of press rights, then, focuses on a variety of "new" media as well as on more traditional media. Specifically, we tested for differences in public willingness to support press rights across the following forms of media: the Internet, magazines, broadcast television, basic cable television, premium subscription cable television, and radio. We also tested the public limits of free press for billboards and video stores.

In testing the public's appetite for supporting freedom of the press across alternative forms of media, it is first necessary to focus on a specific type of media content that is more difficult for the public to accept. If the content involves light local news or the weather, there theoretically exists no logical reason for individuals to deny that or any other medium its right to publish. By contrast, content that is perceived as threatening or offensive might cause the public to back off its support for free press rights on the basis of a qualified competing value judgment. Media differences may become much more apparent under those circumstances.

We selected "sexually explicit material" as a type of media content with which to test the limits of support for freedom of the press across various media forms. In that context, we suspect that (1) the way material is presented by the medium (i.e., printed words versus moving pictures versus printed pictures) might influence willingness to extend press rights; (2) the accessibility of the medium by young people might have an influence; and (3) the extent to which any individual may be passively exposed to the material (as contrasted with the need to actively acquire the material) might have an influence (courts have termed this factor "invasiveness"). For example, sexually explicit written materials in a magazine may be viewed differently from a television show depicting a sexual act. Or the fact that sexual material on broadcast television is more accessible to teens than sexual material on pay cable channels

(because parents can choose not to subscribe to these pay cable channels) may lead individuals to differentiate press rights on that basis. To
give one other example, the unwanted exposure to a sexual act depicted
on a billboard may be viewed quite differently from the same exact depic-
tion in a video that requires active rental or purchase.

Table 5.1 depicts the findings from a battery of items used to measure
differential support for press rights across media. The data indicate that
members of the American public do make significant distinctions across
media in the free press rights they are willing to extend, at least when it
comes to publishing controversial material such as sexually explicit
subject matter. Our hypotheses regarding accessibility of the medium and
passive versus active exposure to the medium do seem to hold some
weight: People appear to distinguish between alternative media in their
willingness to extend press rights. Video store rentals are relatively more
difficult to access and require actively seeking the material (i.e., one must
visit a rental store, pay to rent or purchase a movie, and demonstrate
that he or she is of sufficient age to rent movies rated with sexually
explicit material). Parents enjoy a much greater level of control in allowing their children access to movie rentals than to movies appearing on
television. Also, passive exposure to a rented movie is unlikely and is far
less invasive. It is not surprising, then, that the highest percentage of
Americans (63 percent) agrees that video stores should be allowed to
offer movies containing sexually explicit material.

We find some very significant differences across demographic groups
on the public's willingness to allow video stores to rent sexually explicit
videos. The gender gap, for example, is quite pronounced. Fully 74
percent of men, compared with 54 percent of women, support allowing
video stores the right to rent videos containing sexual material. As
women may be more offended by sexually explicit material than men,
the content we chose to test seems to have the effect of differentiating
the gender groups in terms of their willingness to support press rights.
We find even larger differences between young adults in the eighteen- to
twenty-nine-year-old group and senior citizens. Fully 78 percent of the
younger group (compared with only 38 percent of the older group) supports allowing video stores to rent sexually explicit videos. Interestingly,
about two-thirds of those in age groups between thirty and sixty-one
express similar opinions on this issue.

Knowledge and educational background also exert a substantial influence on these freedoms. Eighty percent of those with high concrete
knowledge about the First Amendment agree that video stores should
be allowed to rent videos with sexual material, compared with only 48
percent of those with low concrete knowledge; and 70 percent of those
who have had a course on the First Amendment support the extension

Table 5.1. Differential Support for Press Rights Across Media

"I'm going to read you some ways people might exercise their First Amendment rights of freedom of the press. For each, please tell me if you strongly agree, mildly agree, mildly disagree, or strongly disagree that someone should be allowed to do it."

	Strongly agree	Mildly agree	Mildly disagree	Strongly disagree
Video stores should be allowed to rent out sexually explicit videos.	24%	39%	9%	25%
Thinking specifically about premium subscription cable channels like HBO, Cinemax, and Showtime, do you think they should be allowed to show sexually explicit material on the air?	25	34	11	28
People should be allowed to publish sexually explicit material in magazines.	16	29	12	41
Radio shows should be allowed to talk about sexually explicit material.	10	22	21	45
People should be allowed to place sexually explicit material on the Internet.	11	19	13	55
Basic cable television should be allowed to show sexually explicit material on the air.	10	16	18	55
Broadcast television, such as networks like NBC and CBS, should be allowed to show sexually explicit material on the air.	6	12	18	64
Advertisers should be allowed to place sexually explicit material on billboards.	3	6	15	76

Note: The items in this battery were randomized to avoid the problem of response set bias.
Source: CSRA University of Connecticut Survey, 1999.

of press rights in this area, compared with 56 percent of those who have not had such a course. Overall level of education also has a large impact, with three-quarters of the college educated compared with 53 percent of those without a college education extending press rights to video rentals. Clearly, more formal education and concrete knowledge of First Amendment issues breed greater appreciation of free expression rights and a greater willingness to extend those rights in potentially controversial circumstances.

A clear majority (59 percent) of Americans is also willing to allow premium subscription channels, such as HBO and Cinemax, the free press rights to air sexually explicit material. These subscription channels are similar to movie rentals in that access is relatively more controlled, and exposure to sexual material is more purposive. Parents may choose not to subscribe to these premium channels, thus denying access to their children and preventing passive exposure. We find similar gaps in public support for the extension of press rights to premium subscription cable channels to those we found with video rentals. Men are 28 points more likely than women, young people are 47 points more likely than seniors, the better educated are 25 points more likely than the lesser educated, and the most knowledgeable are 37 points more likely than the least knowledgeable, to support the right of premium channels to broadcast sexually explicit material.

Interestingly, the public expresses less support for allowing magazines the right to present sexually explicit material than they do for video rentals and premium subscription television stations. Magazines are often purchased or bought on a subscription basis, and so access and passive exposure is more or less limited. This is a particularly interesting finding in light of the differences inherent in the medium. Videos and premium channels provide moving pictures, whereas magazines show only still images. Sexually explicit material in moving pictures thus might be perceived as more threatening than a still picture. Perhaps it is also significant that magazines are thought to be more readily accessible to children than adult videos and premium channels.

Even fewer Americans are willing to extend to radio broadcasters the right to transmit sexually explicit material. Although the medium of radio offers only words and no pictures to its audience, only 32 percent of the public agree that sexually explicit material should be allowed on it. The nature of the medium alone, therefore, does not appear to explain the public's willingness to deny press rights. Rather, access of the public to the medium of radio is significant, which likely explains why few support radio's right to air whatever it wants.

On the medium of radio, we find some significant subgroup differences. There is a gender gap: 42 percent of men, compared with 24 percent of women, support allowing sexually explicit material on the radio. There are also significant differences across age groups, with younger people being more supportive of press rights for radio: eighteen to twenty-nine (44 percent), thirty to sixty-one (32 percent), and sixty-two or older (23 percent). Also, 47 percent of college graduates compared with only 23 percent of those with a high school education are willing to extend press rights to radio. Those with more concrete knowledge of First Amendment issues as well as those identifying themselves as politically liberal also tend to be more pro–press rights.

Likewise, only about three in ten Americans extend the right of transmitting sexually explicit material via the Internet. As we discussed earlier, the Internet, a relatively new medium, is still in its adoption phase in American society. Slightly fewer than half of American households reported having access to the Internet in the spring of 1999.[11] During that same period, more than three-quarters of those between the ages of twelve and nineteen reported having access to the Internet.[12] The growing access to the Internet, particularly among young people,[13] combined with the manner in which information may be presented on it (printed material along with moving pictures), leads most Americans to support denying that medium the rights to publish sexually explicit materials.

Those Americans who use the Internet are much more likely to support press rights for that medium. Specifically, 35 percent of Internet users, compared with 18 percent of non-users, support allowing sexually explicit material on that medium. And as one might expect, those who identify themselves as political conservatives are less supportive (22 percent) of allowing sexually explicit materials on the Internet compared with political moderates (34 percent) and liberals (42 percent). Additionally, having had formal courses on First Amendment topics and having higher levels of concrete knowledge of the First Amendment both have a positive influence on support for extending press rights to the Internet. Thirty-eight percent of those who took First Amendment courses and 51 percent of those with high knowledge levels agree that the Internet should be allowed to publish sexual material, compared with only 22 percent of those with no courses and 12 percent of those with low concrete knowledge. There is a gender gap of 19 percentage points for the medium of the Internet; for magazines, the gender gap is 28 points.

These subgroup differences in support of free press rights apply not only to opinions about the Internet but to other media as well. Across all of the media forms we asked about, conservatives are more likely to disagree that sexually explicit material should be allowed. This is not

---

[11] A survey conducted by CSRA at the University of Connecticut in March 1999 found that 45 percent of U.S. households have access to the Internet.

[12] This finding is from a national survey of 400 teens conducted by the Blue Engine Corp. The survey was conducted in June 1999.

[13] It is interesting to note, however, that those Americans who have children under eighteen living in their household are no more likely to oppose allowing sexually explicit material on the Internet than those who have no children living at home.

surprising given the political constituencies of the contemporary conservative ideology. It is interesting, however, that we find few to no differences when comparing Democrats and Republicans. With respect to publishing sexual material in magazines, for example, 40 percent of Democrats say it should be allowed, compared with 42 percent of Republicans. Interestingly, political independents are most likely to be willing to extend press rights to all media forms. In the case of magazines, fully 54 percent of independents agree that sexual material should be allowed.

We also find that public willingness to extend to the press the right to broadcast sexually explicit materials drops even further when people think about basic cable television (26 percent) and broadcast television (18 percent). These types of television stations are readily accessible to most who own television sets. Further, as we discussed earlier in this chapter, we know that most television viewing involves passive rather than active exposure. It is not surprising, then, that the outlets which provide high accessibility and greater opportunities for passive exposure are also those with relatively lower levels of support for allowing the press to broadcast sexually explicit material.

The discrepancies between demographic groups in their willingness to extend press rights to broadcast and basic cable television are less pronounced than what we found with magazines, the Internet, videos, and premium subscription TV channels. There remains only a very slight tendency for men, younger people, liberals, and the better educated and more knowledgeable to be more supportive of free press rights. In effect, this suggests that there is greater consensus among subgroups that outlets with broad and easy access coupled with opportunities that offer passive exposure should be limited in the material they may broadcast.

A final medium we inquired about was billboards. Billboards are, of course, the most accessible of all media forms we tested and offer the greatest opportunities for passive and unwelcome exposure. Obtaining information from a billboard requires nothing more than being in the right place at the right time. Indeed, billboard opportunities for access and passive exposure have a clear and convincing effect on the public's willingness to allow the publishing of sexually explicit material on that medium. Not surprisingly, fewer than one in ten Americans agree that sexual material should be allowed on billboards. Further, there is clear consensus among demographic groups regarding this opinion, as we find no statistically significant differences among gender, education, or knowledge subgroups.

Clearly the public makes distinctions between types and forms of media in their willingness to allow controversial material to be published or broadcast. But these distinctions are not haphazard or random.

Rather, there appears to be a rationale that the general public applies as it weighs the value of freedom of the press against the appropriateness of material that may be provided through the media. With regard to media that allow for broad and open access, as well as provide opportunities for passive exposure, the public is less inclined to support press rights when the material presented is deemed potentially inappropriate. However, for media that provide greater control of access and that require actively seeking out the material, the public is much more willing to extend the rights of the press, even though the material may be less socially acceptable.

Indeed, the collective response of the public demonstrates a reasoned and rational approach to the application of free press rights. The capacity of the masses to apply a rational approach is on a par with the legal rationale applied by the courts. These findings suggest that earlier research, which characterized the public as fickle and prone to disregarding support for rights in the abstract when faced with negative concrete situations, may not have given the masses enough credit for their abilities to engage in sophisticated thinking.

Public Support for the Internet

Perhaps more than anything else, the technology of the Internet provides the greatest challenges to freedom of the press in contemporary society. As was discussed earlier in this chapter, the Internet expands the definition of "the press" to include anyone with a computer and an Internet connection. Freedom of the press thus becomes a privilege that virtually anyone in the public can claim, not merely a right belonging to organizations in the more mainstream, established media or to individuals employed by those media.

As has already been discussed, only about three in ten Americans would allow the publishing of sexually explicit material on the Internet. As a medium, this ranks well below the numbers of Americans who are willing to allow the broadcasting of sexually explicit material on home videos, on premium subscription cable stations, and in magazines. Still, more in the public are willing to allow the Internet the right to publish sexual material than are willing to extend this press right to basic cable, broadcast television, and billboards. The public's concerns about who may access the Internet (in particular, young people) drive down willingness to support press rights. But the nature of exposure to material on the Internet is that the user must actively pursue it, and so passive exposure is unlikely.

One method of allowing parents more control in determining the kind of materials their children can access would be a system of rating Internet sites. Such a ratings system might be used to help parents decide which sites they choose to "block out" on a home computer. The ratings system may be similar to the system that is currently used for entertainment television programs. This issue raises a number of questions relating to the concept of freedom of the press. Most central is the question about whether or not the government should have a role in developing such a system. Public support for government intervention could conceivably contribute to limiting the rights of those publishing material on the Internet. We asked our national sample of Americans what they thought about giving the government a role in developing a ratings system for Internet material and found that a majority in the general public believes the government should be involved in some fashion. Specifically, 58 percent of Americans say that government should be involved in developing a system, while 37 percent say that government should not be involved.

Interestingly, public support for government involvement in a ratings system for the Internet parallels support for government involvement in developing a ratings system for entertainment television programming and for television news programming. Specifically, 57 percent say that government should be involved in rating entertainment programming, and 59 percent say the government should be involved in rating news programming. Indeed, the public does not appear to distinguish (as the courts clearly have) between the medium of television and the medium of the Internet in terms of the regulatory role that government might assume. But while the public may be generally supportive of a government role in developing ratings systems for various media, we also found that a majority (53 percent) of the public rejects the idea that government should be allowed to regulate what appears in the media. Sixty-four percent of the public believes that giving government the power to decide which TV programs can or cannot be shown violates the public's right to watch what it pleases.

In both 1997 and 1999, we asked the public about the Supreme Court's decision in *Reno v. ACLU*, inquiring as to whether it agreed that the broad First Amendment protections traditionally given to books and newspapers should be extended to the Internet. A majority of the general public appeared to be sympathetic to the Court's majority opinion. Specifically, in the 1999 survey we found that nearly two-thirds either strongly (31 percent) or mildly (33 percent) agreed with the ruling that material on the Internet should have the same broad protections as printed material such as books and newspapers. Less than one-third either strongly (14 percent) or mildly (17 percent) disagreed with extending broad press protections to the Internet. Those who use the Internet and are thus more familiar with it are most supportive of extending to the Internet the rights that members of the print press normally enjoy.

More than two-thirds of Internet users, compared with 54 percent of non-users, agree that the Internet should have broad First Amendment protections. We also find a proclivity for the better educated and those with more concrete knowledge of the First Amendment to be more supportive of broad press rights for the Internet, again confirming the notion that knowledge and education breed support for the value of a free press in U.S. society.

Public Support for Other Media Forms

As we discussed earlier in this chapter, there are a wide variety of media through which information and opinions can be communicated. The more traditional conceptualization of "free press" was limited to news organizations and reporters transmitting the news through television, newspapers, magazines, and radio. Yet views are commonly expressed through other media, such as books, music, and art, and so a broader notion of what might be considered the press must include those media as well. Those who use these media to express their ideas might also stake a legitimate claim to the freedom of the press rights guaranteed by the First Amendment.

Survey data show that the public is willing to extend press rights to the medium of books under certain controversial circumstances, but not under others. Respondents were asked to choose between the following two statements: (1) "Novels that describe explicit sex acts have no place in a school library and should be banned" and (2) "Novels that describe explicit sex acts should be permitted in the library if they are worthwhile literature." Fifty-six percent said they should be permitted, while 38 percent said they should be banned. On the other hand, when asked to respond to "Do you think that books that could show how to build bombs should be banned from public libraries or available in the library like every other book?" 58 percent say they should be banned while 37 percent say they should be available. While the public is willing to extend press freedoms to books in libraries where the content might be controversial, it is not willing to extend those same rights when the public safety may be jeopardized. This confirms the qualification hypothesis to a degree. When the value of a free press is pitted against the value of limiting sexual materials to youth, press values win out. However, when free press values compete with the value of safety and security, the latter prevails.

Music and art are two other forms of media that might claim press rights. With respect to these two media, we again found mixed results in terms of the public's willingness to extend press rights under various circumstances. For example, when asked if they agreed or disagreed that "Musicians should be allowed to sing songs with words that others might find offensive," 56 percent agreed and 41 percent disagreed. However, when asked whether they agreed or disagreed with "People should be allowed to display in a public place art that has content that may be offensive to others," only 41 percent agreed, while 57 percent disagreed. While a majority of the public is willing to extend rights to those expressing views, even those that might offend, through the medium of music, a similar majority is not willing to extend rights to those expressing potentially offensive views through the medium of art.

CONCLUSION

When attempting to define pornography for constitutional purposes in one case, the late Justice Potter Stewart famously quipped: "I can't define it, but I know it when I see it."[14] At first glance, it might seem as if the courts and the American public have adopted a similar seat-of-the-pants approach to determining what types of press organizations are worthy of constitutional protection and which ones should not be accorded such privileges. Rather than simply define one "freedom of the press" that applies to all, the Supreme Court has often distinguished between the right to publish printed materials and the right to broadcast. Similarly, the public has refused to back similar levels of freedom for newspapers, television, movies, and even the Internet. What we find today is a confusing patchwork quilt of degrees of protection for various media, the bulk of which enjoy considerable public support.

Ironically, although the courts and the public have reached many of the same conclusions, they arrived at those conclusions by following unique paths that only occasionally overlap. The Supreme Court's focus over the past half-century has been primarily on the problem of "technological scarcity": Are there too few outlets of communication for too many potential speakers? Thus radio and television have never enjoyed the same level of constitutional protection afforded to the print media because government regulation may be required to protect the so-called "marketplace of ideas" in those contexts. While even the most oppressed members of society may enjoy some access to publish their ideas in written form, they still may be denied access to the free television audience absent some forms of government intervention. By this reasoning, cable television and the Internet should enjoy relatively high levels of protection because the "technological scarcity" argument seems less applicable in those contexts. Meanwhile, levels of invasiveness remain a secondary concern for the courts. Certainly, in *Reno v. ACLU*, the Supreme Court expressed interest in how these new media inject

[14] *Jacobellis v. Ohio*, 378 U.S. 184, 197 (1964).

themselves into our homes without our permission. But as the press-protective outcome of that decision suggests, technological scarcity and the access to publish continue to dominate the Court's reasoning.

Understandably, the public's obsession lies not so much with access of publishers to publish as with the access of the audience to see *what has already been published.* In other words, the public appears most willing to accept restrictions on the freedom of the press when those restrictions assist us in voluntarily "averting our eyes." Those media that feature more graphic displays of sex, violence, or other controversial materials (free and other forms of cable television and the Internet) receive relatively low degrees of support, except for those instances in which considerable effort is necessary to attain access (e.g., subscription channels such as HBO).

Perhaps the Court is simply keeping an eye on public opinion, or maybe it has stumbled upon a position that is genuinely quite popular. There may also be a reverse cause-effect at work, with Supreme Court opinions actually shaping public opinion. No matter the direction, the current state of constitutional protection lies relatively near the prevailing public sentiment. Indeed, the most notable exception to this congruence may be the Internet. A clear majority of the public favors restrictions on Internet publishing freedom on the theory that it is too easily accessible by the audience.

By contrast, the Court in recent years has subscribed to the notion that the Internet should be treated like newspapers and magazines for purposes of constitutional protection, on grounds that there is no technological scarcity in that medium. Such a discrepancy may represent a real source of concern for libertarians, as public sentiment for regulating the Internet continues to gather steam. Those supporters of expansive press freedoms should take heart in other respects, however. The public's support for press freedoms does not amount to a haphazard cacophony of anger and hostility against the general freedom to publish, as earlier research suggested. Rather, the public appears to have adopted a sophisticated approach toward press freedoms, focusing on the priority to keep graphic materials away from those who don't want to see them, or who don't want their children to see them. The reservoir of good will toward the right to publish remains quite strong. And as we will see in Chapter 6, the public has refused to let personalities or its general distaste for particular members of the media undermine its fundamental understanding of the importance of press freedoms in a democracy.

6

Support for Press Freedoms within a Medium:
Elite, Mainstream, and Tabloid News Sources

One would be hard pressed to find two newspapers with more contrasting styles and reputations than the *New York Times* and the now-defunct *Saturday Press* of Minneapolis, Minnesota. The former, a nationally recognized institution, has worked hard over the past century and a half to establish its reputation as perhaps the premier "newspaper of record" in the United States. With a daily circulation that numbers in the millions, the *Times* takes seriously its power to influence political agendas at both the local and national levels. And the *Times*'s editors have long preached adherence to rigorous journalistic standards, ever loyal to the paper's slogan that it publish "all the news that's fit to print." By contrast, the *Saturday Press*, first produced during the late 1920s, was considered by many at that time to be a scurrilous and flamboyant newspaper – far more equipped to provoke public outrage than to provide an objective version of the facts. Owned by the racist, anti-Semitic, and anti-Catholic publisher Jay Near, the *Saturday Press* continually leveled charges of corruption against Minneapolis city leaders. Although often lacking clear evidence to support its accusations, the paper relentlessly attacked local officials, referring to them in many instances as outright "gangsters" (Friendly, 1981). And while many of Near's charges about corruption-ridden Minneapolis turned out to be prophetic, he remained a pariah in his community.

As different as these two newspapers would appear on their face, both played important roles in shaping First Amendment jurisprudence during the past century. The *New York Times* was a central litigant in a number of important constitutional cases, including *New York Times v. Sullivan* (discussed in Chapter 1) and the high-visibility Pentagon Papers case of 1971, *New York Times v. United States*.[1] In the latter case, the U.S. Supreme Court denied the government's request for an injunction

---

[1] *New York Times Co. v. United States*, 403 U.S. 713 (1971).

restraining the *New York Times* and the *Washington Post* from publishing purloined classified war documents commissioned by the Johnson administration. The government had claimed that publication of the documents would provide the enemy with helpful information. But the Court believed that the federal government had not met the "heavy burden" of justifying a prior restraint in the case. And while Justice Byron White's concurrence suggested numerous ways the government might choose to hold those newspapers liable *after* publication – including possible criminal prosecution for illegally publishing "classified information"[2] – the government ultimately pursued none of those options. Nothing short of a restraint on publication would satisfy the federal government, and that possibility had been effectively foreclosed by the majority's holding.

In the Pentagon Papers case, both sides were wrestling with the scope and application of a four-decades-old Supreme Court precedent, *Near v. Minnesota*.[3] In that case, the aforementioned *Saturday Press* faced charges that its brand of scandal mongering had violated a local public nuisance law. The law in question authorized the abatement of any "malicious, scandalous and defamatory newspaper, or other periodical." Rejecting the authorities' attempt to close down the newspaper under the statute, Chief Justice Charles Evans Hughes declared for a split court in *Near* that the First Amendment protects the press against prior restraint in all but the most exceptional of circumstances. Eventually it became clear that the Pentagon Papers case would not be considered such an exception. Together, these two cases contributed significantly to the modern landscape of First Amendment law by reaffirming the Blackstonian premise that pre-publication review enjoys little or no place in a free society. That they could spring from lawsuits pressed by two such markedly different publications is a testament to the power of the freedom of the press and its broad scope.

The United States' legacy of protection for even the least reputable or disrespected of publications dates back to the founding. Thomas Jefferson was hardly a fan of the many newspapers that dominated early American political life, deploring the "putrid state into which our newspapers have passed . . . and the mendacious spirit of those who write for them."[4] To James Monroe, Jefferson complained of "printers raven on the agonies of their victims, as wolves do on the blood of the lamb."[5]

---

[2] 403 U.S. at 733–7 (White, J., concurring).
[3] *Near v. Minnesota*, 283 U.S. 697 (1931).
[4] Thomas Jefferson to Walter Jones, 1814. A. A. Lipscomb and A. E. Bergh, eds., *The Writings of Thomas Jefferson, Memorial Edition* (Washington, D.C., 1903–4), 14:46.
[5] Thomas Jefferson to James Monroe, 1811. *Writings of Thomas Jefferson*, 13:59.

But even though Jefferson viewed the United States as a country "afraid to read nothing," he remained convinced that the public should be "trusted with anything, so long as its reason remains unfettered by law."[6]

In the late twentieth century this fundamental credo was tested in new and innovative ways. Sensational newspapers such as the *Star* and the *National Enquirer* were driven not so much by journalistic principles or ideological agendas as by the single-minded economic goal of attracting a larger audience. The sexual revolution of the 1960s and 1970s pushed the envelope on the types of graphic, sexually explicit materials available to consumers from printed and broadcast news sources. Daytime television features crass displays of human behavior on talk shows like "The Jerry Springer Show." And thanks to the Internet, the *New York Times* and independent computer hackers enjoy nearly comparable technological power to disseminate information electronically to the greater public. As Chapter 5 made clear, differences among media forms certainly have an impact on the levels of protection they receive under the First Amendment. But should different sources within the same medium type be afforded equal levels of constitutional protection? Without sufficient support from both the legal system and the public as a whole, publishers that fall outside the mainstream or elite press may not enjoy the discretion to publish that is considered so central to their continued free existence.

"OUT OF THE MAINSTREAM": EQUAL PROTECTION FOR EVERY NEWS SOURCE?

Anyone can report the news. Although technological scarcity in some cases requires that the limited number of television and radio frequencies be fairly distributed, the government does not issue press "licenses," nor does it provide for regulatory procedures that all news organizations and reporters must follow. Its failure to do so may be grounded in both theoretical and pragmatic concerns. How does one go about setting news industry standards that are consistent with the First Amendment's guarantee of a "freedom of the press"? In *New York Times v. Sullivan*, the Supreme Court recognized the intrinsic value of even some false information. Stated simply, as a society we must often put up with inaccuracies on the part of the press (especially when reporting on public officials) because we don't want to unnecessarily chill such commentary in the first place.

The legal system thus encourages news organizations to aggressively report on public figures, even if this means increasing the risk that false

---

[6] Thomas Jefferson to Joseph Milligan, 1816. *Writings of Thomas Jefferson*, 14:463.

information is disseminated. Given the premise of this legal framework, how can one dismiss as invaluable or irrelevant the many press organizations that maintain only poor reputations for reporting the truth? Even though a number of journalism schools have established formidable reputations in recent years, many of the United States' most respected reporters have never received any formal training in their field (Medsger, 1996). ABC's Peter Jennings, like some other respected journalists, never attended college. The government routinely requires that public school teachers, lawyers, and physicians meet certification standards as a prerequisite to practicing their respective vocations. By contrast, no objective method exists to distinguish those reporters and press organizations (print or otherwise) that deserve more constitutional protection from those that deserve less.

Naturally, citizens differentiate between news sources every day when they turn on the television or read the newspaper. Reports from news organizations or outlets with reputations for being more truthful are more likely to be accepted at face value; sensational news shows or publications are more likely to be viewed as "entertainment" – perhaps to be enjoyed but not necessarily to be trusted. In a recent study, the public indicated that it trusts local TV news anchors slightly more than it trusts network TV anchors and far more than it trusts radio talk show hosts.[7] As a substantive matter, there is little basis for the public to make such across-the-board judgments in favor of local newscasts; as one scholar recently put it, people often "lambaste the generic [press] industry for behavior commonly found on the very outlets they watch" (Sanford, 1999:23–4). Nor do such distinctions have any legal significance per se. Citizens here are making *content-based* distinctions, favoring or disfavoring publications and broadcasts based on the nature and style by which they convey information.

Are all content-based legal distinctions illegitimate? At the heart of First Amendment jurisprudence lies the fundamental tenet that government may not suppress, control, or even penalize particular ideas or information on the basis of viewpoint. Accordingly, the U.S. legal system guards strenuously against any efforts to regulate communications simply because the views or information contained therein are not welcome. There are some well-established exceptions to this strict ban

---

[7] Specifically, 53 percent of the respondents indicated either that they trust "most" or "all" of what local television news anchors say, compared with 45 percent for network television anchors and 15 percent for radio talk show hosts. See "Americans' Views of the News: What They Like, What They Don't Like, and What Sources They Use," Study Sponsored by the Freedom Forum, conducted by the Roper Center for Public Opinion Research, University of Connecticut, February 1997.

on content-based regulations. In *Chaplinsky v. New Hampshire* (1942),[8] the U.S. Supreme Court singled out certain categories of speech as not warranting First Amendment protection because their "very utterance inflicts injury."[9] Included on that list were "the lewd and obscene, the profane, the libelous, and the insulting or 'fighting words.'"[10] Thus, for example, any effort to ban or discriminate against truly "obscene" materials may theoretically represent a legitimate governmental interest.

But distinctions between "reputable" and "less reputable" press organizations do not align themselves so neatly into any one of those traditionally "unprotected" categories. Depending on the particular nature of the news of the day, the NBC evening news with Tom Brokaw may transmit information on a number of subjects that make its audience uncomfortable, including frank discussions of sex and violence. One particular episode of "The Jerry Springer Show" may carefully edit out all references or incidents that cross the line into the legal definition of "obscene." Can one say with any real confidence that Tom Brokaw's broadcast deserves more "newsgathering protection" and discretion to publish than does Jerry Springer's broadcast? Today's sensational tabloid may become tomorrow's voice of reason – attempts to distinguish between worthy and unworthy newspapers are particularly precarious undertakings.

A central question thus remains: Do Americans distinguish among the different outlets in the amount of constitutional freedom they should receive? At least three different types of media have been identified in this context.

- *Mainstream media outlets* are defined as those that fall within the prevailing patterns of readership or listenership. Television's predominance as a source of news in this country places CBS, NBC, and ABC at the heart of the so-called mainstream today. During the Persian Gulf War in early 1991, CNN arguably cemented its position in the mainstream for the foreseeable future. Local television newscasts also garner a high level of public use (Dautrich and Hartley, 1999). And local newspapers enjoy the next highest degree of interest, placing them squarely within the mainstream of public consumption. Moreover, news magazines such as *Time* and *Newsweek* are not just for news junkies anymore; they draw a readership base that crosses many sectors and demographic groups in society.
- *Elite media outlets* generally supplement the more limited-in-scope, maintream news provided by network and local television news

---

[8] 315 U.S. 568 (1942).   [9] Id. at 571–2.   [10] Id.

broadcasts, as well as local print news. In-depth and comprehensive information may be available in national newspapers such as the *New York Times* and the *Wall Street Journal*, as well as through elite radio and television news broadcasts such as "The News Hour with Jim Lehrer," NPR (National Public Radio), and the plethora of Sunday morning talk shows (Popkin, 1991). These outlets concern themselves less with expanding their audience at any cost and more with providing substantive analysis of issues that is not ordinarily available to the public, precisely because of those economic constraints. The proliferation of cable news channels and the Internet has given these elite media outlets greater access to the public, despite their limited economic upside. C-SPAN and Court TV in particular are two elite news outlets that now reach a substantial majority of American households. Elite news magazines such as *The New Republic* and *The Nation* are now joined in the political dialogue by elite Internet publications such as *Slate* and *Salon*, available to the public free of charge.

• *Tabloid media outlets* attempt to drum up large niche audiences by covering subjects that are interesting, rather than simply newsworthy, with regard to the public interest. Accordingly, they usually provide little if any reliable political information, focusing instead on entertainment or human interest news. Tabloid news sources include television shows such as "Inside Edition" and "Hard Copy," and newspapers such as the *National Enquirer* or the *Star*. None of these "news sources" strives to maintain the same reputations for accuracy and thoroughness as do many of the mainstream or elite providers.

Of course, many news organizations do not fit readily into any of these categories. *Hustler* magazine, for example, is not really a "tabloid" news source, but it does provide information to a specific niche of reader. Cable television news shows like those on the Fox News channel or MSNBC have tried to break into the mainstream, but their proper place in this framework remains at least arguable. Small, independent Internet publishers such as Matt Drudge are often grouped in as part of the "tabloid" press, but Drudge's appearances for a short period in 1999 on Fox News and ABC radio may render him part of the "mainstream" or even "elite" media in the views of some.

Certainly the public views all of these various organizations – as well as the news and information that they provide – with varying degrees of suspicion and trust. But does it also support having varying levels of constitutional protection for outlets that maintain such different reputations for quality? An answer in the affirmative might well lead us to question the distinctions the public often makes across media types, as we identified in Chapter 5. Specifically, if the public affords far less protection to a tabloid newspaper than the *New York Times*, then issues of invasiveness and access (theoretically the same in both instances) may not hold the same high level of importance in the public's mind than was originally hypothesized. Even more crucially, the reservoir of good will we have discovered toward the freedom of the press will have sprung a significant leak – one that may be particularly difficult to patch given the proliferation of sensational publishers and low-quality media institutions during the 1990s.

SUPPORT FOR PRESS RIGHTS WITHIN EACH MEDIUM: A RATIONAL PUBLIC?

As we discussed in the previous chapter, the American public appears to make clear, rational distinctions among the press rights they are willing to extend to different media. The most invasive and easily accessible forms of media receive the least freedom to publish/broadcast, while the least invasive and more difficult-to-access media are given the most freedom. This rational balancing act by the public accounts for the need to allow the press to fulfill its important roles in the U.S. democratic system and at the same time protects individuals from exposure to unwanted and/or undesirable material.

If the public is truly rational when it comes to support for press freedoms, one might expect that same public to refuse to distinguish among specific outlets within a medium in support of press freedoms. For example, if a majority of the public believes that newspapers should have the freedom to publish a particular kind of story, and that decision is based on rational criteria (such as level of invasiveness of the medium or ease of access of the medium), then the public should be willing to extend the same press rights to all newspapers. In other words, the specific outlet within a medium should not dictate the freedom to publish or broadcast, as outlets within a medium offer similar non-content-based characteristics in terms of invasiveness and access.

Given the wide variety of outlets that exist within any one medium in the current media environment, this is a relatively easy hypothesis to test. Within the category of newspapers, for example, one can easily identify popular and well-recognized "elite" outlets, such as the *New York Times* and the *Wall Street Journal*, as well as the less reputable "tabloid" outlets, such as the *National Enquirer* and the *Star*. Similarly, within the category of magazines one can find news outlets such as *Newsweek*, *Time*, and *Business Week*, along with *Playboy* and *Hustler*. There is a wide spectrum of outlets within television news programming as well, ranging from traditional news programs such as "ABC World News

Tonight" and "CNN Headline News" to tabloid news programming like "The Jerry Springer Show" and "The Jenny Jones Show." And between each of these extremes exists considerable variety.

The public's orientation toward these outlets offering very different types of content is likely to vary. For example, Dautrich and Hartley (1999) found differences in public trust and confidence in election news across specific outlets within the medium of television (pp. 110–11). Just et al. (1996) found that the nature of the news environment has changed dramatically since the 1970s and that much of that change was the result of the explosion of news outlets across these various forms of media.

Our analysis in this chapter, then, addresses whether the American public makes distinctions between outlets within a medium in the press rights it is willing to support. If the public is indeed applying a "content neutral" rationale across media when it supports extending different levels of press freedoms to different media forms, invasiveness and ease of access should be the primary factors that generate public hostility. This "content neutral" approach does not, however, justify differences across specific outlets within a medium. If the American public is willing to extend similar press freedoms across a wide variety of outlets that produce very different content, one may conclude that support for freedom of the press is alive and well. Is the public willing to support basic press freedoms even when it disapproves of the content published by an outlet?

The "Slippery Slope" Argument

If the public does apply a "content neutral" rationale to allowing press freedoms across media, it should likewise apply this rationale within outlets in a particular medium. Limiting freedoms of a particular outlet, based on content, opens the door to a slippery slope: Once government limits freedoms of a particular outlet based on content, it becomes much easier to limit freedoms of other outlets. We thus included an item in our 1997 survey to measure the extent to which the public understood and appreciated the "slippery slope" argument. Responses to the item indicate that the American public is quite sympathetic to the slippery slope argument, at least in principle. Fully 84 percent of the public agrees that once government starts limiting certain rights, it becomes much easier to put limits on more rights – and as many as two-thirds of all Americans "strongly" agree with this premise (see Figure 6.1).

There is good reason to believe, then, that the public may indeed conceptualize the importance of extending the same level of press freedom to outlets within a particular medium, regardless of support for or opposition to the content provided by those various outlets. If the public is supportive of "equal press rights" within a medium, that buttresses the

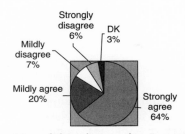

Figure 6.1. Public recognition of the "slippery slope" argument. **"Do you agree or disagree with the following statement: Once the government starts limiting certain rights it becomes easier to put limits on more rights."** (Source: CSRA University of Connecticut Survey, 1997.)

argument that it applies a rational approach to free press rights in U.S. society. And it suggests that press freedoms are strongly supported by the masses, despite the well-documented disdain for the performance of the contemporary press in the United States. We now specifically address the question of whether or not the public differentiates between outlets within a medium in the rights it is willing to extend.

Within-Medium Differentiation in Support of Press Rights

To measure the level of public support for extending freedom of the press to all outlets within a medium, we administered a series of three items. One item dealt with newspapers, the second focused on magazines, and the third looked at television programming. Each of the items identified several outlets within the medium, with one of the outlets a more traditional, respected outlet and the other a more controversial outlet. The items asked respondents if the controversial outlet should have the same freedom to publish/broadcast as the more traditional outlet. For the item on newspapers, the traditional outlets selected were the *New York Times* and the *Wall Street Journal*, and the more controversial outlets were the *Star* and the *National Enquirer*. For magazines, we selected *Time* and *Newsweek* for the traditional and *Hustler* and *Playboy* for the controversial. Finally, for TV we picked "ABC News with Peter Jennings" (traditional) and "The Jerry Springer Show" and "The Jenny Jones Show" (controversial).

If the general public is supportive of the extension of press rights from the traditional outlet to the controversial outlet for the item, then we hypothesize that the public recognizes freedom of the press on a content-neutral basis. On the other hand, if the general public is not willing to extend the same freedom to publish to the *National Enquirer*, for example, as it is to the *New York Times*, then it is clear that distinctions within a medium are being made on the basis of the nature and/or format of the material produced by the specific outlet. We now examine our findings on these three items.

Newspapers

The items testing "within medium" support for newspapers were included on both the 1997 and 1999 surveys. As indicated in Table 6.1, in both years the American public was quite supportive of extending the same press rights afforded to the elite outlets of the *New York Times* and the *Wall Street Journal* to the more controversial tabloids the *Star* and the *National Enquirer.* In 1997, 76 percent of the public agreed that the tabloid newspapers should have the same freedoms to publish what they want as do the elite national newspapers, and in 1999, 71 percent agreed with this statement. Only 22 percent in 1997 and 27 percent in 1999 disagreed with the idea of extending the same press rights to the tabloid newspapers. Indeed, the data from the item show a strong propensity for Americans to grant the same press freedoms to all news-papers, regardless of content and format. High support for extension of press rights, given the extreme polar examples used in the item, adds even more credence to the finding that Americans do tend to favor the content-neutral approach to extending press freedoms.

The overall large-scale support for extending press rights to all news-papers masks some very interesting differences across demographic groups. As Table 6.1 shows, there is a gender gap. Men are 14 percent-age points more likely than women to believe that the tabloid and elite newspapers should have the same press freedoms. Also, higher levels of education produce greater support for extending press freedoms from elite newspapers to tabloid publications, as does increased knowledge of contemporary First Amendment issues. Again, this clearly confirms the positive impact of education and knowledge on public support for the principles of freedom of the press. The effects of knowledge are partic-ularly striking, with 84 percent of the high-knowledge group, compared with 62 percent of the low-knowledge group, willing to extend to the tabloid newspapers the same press rights as enjoyed by the elite publications.

We also find significant differences across ideological groups. Those self-identifying as politically liberal (75 percent) and moderate (77 percent) tend to be more supportive of being content neutral than those who claim to be politically conservative (65 percent). It is important to emphasize, however, that even two-thirds of conservatives are willing to extend equal press rights to all newspapers. Finally, we note some geo-graphic differences. Those living in the western portion of the United

Table 6.1. Support for Press Rights in Different Newspapers

"I'm going to read some ways that people might exercise their First Amendment rights. For each, please tell me if you agree or disagree that someone should be allowed to do it. First: Tabloid newspapers such as the *Star* and the *National Enquirer* should have the same freedom to publish what they want as other newspapers such as the *New York Times* and the *Wall Street Journal*."

	Strongly agree	Mildly agree	Mildly disagree	Strongly disagree
Full sample 1997	43%	33%	8%	14%
Full sample 1999	36	35	8	19
Gender:				
Men	45	33	7	14
Women	28	36	8	24
Education:				
High school	32	34	6	25
Some college	36	35	12	15
College	45	36	6	11
First Amendment knowledge:				
Low	30	32	10	22
Medium–low	30	39	6	23
Medium–high	42	31	7	19
High	48	36	7	8
Political ideology:				
Liberal	41	34	9	14
Moderate	41	36	8	14
Conservative	32	33	6	28
Region:				
Northeast	31	32	10	24
Midwest	36	38	9	15
South	32	37	6	23
West	49	29	7	13

Source: CSRA University of Connecticut Surveys, 1997 and 1999.

States (78 percent) are most apt to support press freedoms for all newspapers regardless of content.

Magazines

With respect to the class of outlets that may be described as magazines, we find similar results. Again, the public appears willing to apply a content-neutral approach when thinking about press freedoms within a

Table 6.2. Support for Press Rights in Different Magazines

"I'm going to read some ways that people might exercise their First Amendment rights. For each, please tell me if you agree or disagree that someone should be allowed to do it. Next: Magazines such as *Playboy* and *Hustler* should have the same freedom to publish what they want as other magazines such as *Time* and *Newsweek*."

	Strongly agree	Mildly agree	Mildly disagree	Strongly disagree
Full sample 1999	39%	32%	7%	20%
Gender:				
Men	51	33	6	10
Women	28	32	8	29
Age:				
18–29	47	29	7	16
30–44	43	33	5	17
45–61	37	35	7	18
62 or older	22	32	9	32
Education:				
High school	31	32	6	27
Some college	44	33	8	13
College	49	33	6	11
First Amendment knowledge:				
Low	27	30	9	30
Medium–low	32	36	7	24
Medium–high	47	31	7	15
High	55	33	5	5
Political ideology:				
Liberal	49	33	5	11
Moderate	43	32	8	16
Conservative	32	33	7	27
Region:				
Northeast	39	31	9	18
Midwest	38	34	8	18
South	33	32	6	27
West	51	31	5	11

Source: CSRA University of Connectiuct Survey, 1999.

particular medium. As is seen in Table 6.2, seven in ten (71 percent) Americans believe that *Playboy* and *Hustler* magazines should have the same freedom to publish what they want as *Time* and *Newsweek* magazines. Fewer than one-third (27 percent) disagree with extending press rights equally within the category of magazines. Again, the extreme examples used in the item – the generally well-regarded news magazines *Time* and *Newsweek* and the sexually explicit *Hustler* – add even more credibility to this finding.

For the magazine item, we find an even larger gender gap than what we found for the newspapers item, with men being nearly 25 percentage points more likely than women to agree that press freedoms should apply equally to all magazines. The specific examples of controversial magazines that we used in this item both dealt with sexually explicit material. It is not surprising, then, that the nature of the content in *Hustler* and *Playboy* would be considered more controversial to women than men and thus drives, at least in part, the large gender gap on this question. We also detect significant differences based on age classification, with younger Americans more likely to support equal press rights. Again, as younger people are less likely to be offended by the sexually explicit nature of the examples in the item, these differences may be in part based on our use of *Hustler* and *Playboy* in the item to represent controversial magazines.

As with the newspapers item, we also confirm that education and knowledge exert an important influence on an individual's propensity to support the content-neutral application of press rights for outlets within a medium. More than four in five with a college degree, and nearly nine in ten who have high levels of knowledge about First Amendment issues, support equal press rights for all magazines. Once again, those who are better educated and more knowledgeable are extremely supportive of freedom of the press, regardless of the nature or content of the specific magazine. Finally, we find, as we did with magazines, that liberals and moderates are more likely than conservatives to support equal press freedoms for all magazines, and that those who live in the West tend to be more supportive than those living in other parts of the country.

Television

We also find majority support for the notion that the public largely adheres to a content-neutral approach in support of press freedoms for television programming. However, public support for extension of press rights for TV outlets is not quite as strong as for the print outlets of newspapers and magazines. Table 6.3 shows that six in ten Americans agree that controversial shows such as those hosted by Jerry Springer and Jenny Jones should have the same freedom to air what they want as shows such as "ABC News with Peter Jennings."

Thirty-seven percent disagree that the same press freedoms should apply to these very different types of programs. While there appears to be at least some distinctions the public is willing to make between print

Table 6.3. Support for Press Rights in Different TV Outlets

"I'm going to read some ways that people might exercise their First Amendment rights. For each, please tell me if you agree or disagree that someone should be allowed to do it. Next: Television programs such as 'The Jerry Springer Show' and 'The Jenny Jones Show' should have the same freedom to air what they want as 'ABC News with Peter Jennings.' "

	Strongly agree	Mildly agree	Mildly disagree	Strongly disagree
Full sample 1999	30%	30%	11%	26%
Gender:				
Men	38	34	10	16
Women	22	27	12	35
Age:				
18–29	39	37	9	14
30–44	34	29	14	22
45–61	25	30	9	33
62 or older	18	26	10	38
Education:				
High school	24	30	11	32
Some college	35	31	11	21
College	38	30	11	18
Had First Amendment course:				
Yes	34	34	11	19
No	26	26	10	34
First Amendment knowledge:				
Low	22	28	10	35
Medium–low	23	28	17	29
Medium–high	39	30	8	22
High	39	38	6	15
Political ideology:				
Liberal	39	35	9	15
Moderate	32	32	12	23
Conservative	25	30	10	32
Region:				
Northeast	30	26	13	27
Midwest	27	33	11	28
South	27	31	11	29
West	39	31	9	18

Source: CSRA University of Connecticut Survey, 1999.

and television in its willingness to apply press rights equally within a medium, it is important to recognize that strong majorities, at least in the instances of newspapers, magazines, and television, are supportive of a content-neutral approach to issuing press freedoms within a medium.

Consistent with our findings from the newspapers and magazines items, gender gap and age differences are also identifiable, in the expected direction, on the television item. We also see consistent findings for the level of education and knowledge of the First Amendment groupings, ideological groups, and regional differences.

CONCLUSION

In Chapter 5 we discovered a public that was anxious to differentiate between highly invasive, overly accessible media on one hand, and less accessible media on the other hand. The former – which included television, radio, and the Internet – were deemed by the public less worthy of constitutional protection; the latter (books, magazines, etc.) were deemed more deserving of such protection. In drawing such a distinction, the public was hardly being irrational – apparently, citizens recognize and accept a greater role for government in regulating press organizations that retain the capacity to overcome normal barriers of entrance into the home. Because a "raunchy" television show or a graphic Web site can be transmitted into the home, often with little or no warning to the passive consumer, they warrant more regulations than print media that must be actively purchased or acquired.

But just how committed is the public to these principles of differentiation among various media? On their face, the distinctions described appear to be "content neutral" – having less to do with the substance and character of the materials than with the manner in which they are disseminated. Thus in theory, *all* newspapers and print media should enjoy equal levels of constitutional protection, and *all* television shows should be afforded similar (albeit lesser) degrees of protection from government intervention. Certainly some types of communications (obscenity, fighting words, libel of private persons, etc.) fall outside the protection of the First Amendment, and any press organization that crosses those lines may be subject to legal consequences. Yet assuming that those minimal standards of protection are not crossed, news organizations of varying reputation and prestige within the same general medium should theoretically be treated equally. In short, a truly rational public should be able to put aside its prejudices toward and disgust with individual reporters and press organizations in making such judgments; otherwise, it risks undercutting the support it claims to maintain. Support for press freedoms that is at once a mile wide and an inch deep may not be so valuable at all.

From this perspective, the public appears to pass the test of rationality with flying colors. As we've already noted, respondents were asked to compare the most controversial news outlets with those from the same medium that are highly respected in most circles. An overwhelming percentage of the public agreed that (1) tabloid newspapers should enjoy the same freedom to publish as elite national newspapers; (2) sexually explicit magazines should enjoy the same level of protection as national news magazines; and (3) controversial and sensational television shows should enjoy the same level of protection as mainstream national news broadcasts. Along with these findings, we also discovered a number of important demographic patterns in support within various media. Men are more likely than women to extend constitutional protection across the board. The same is true for those with higher levels of education, those with above-average knowledge of First Amendment law, and those who identify themselves as politically liberal or moderate.

Based on the combined findings in Chapters 5 and 6, we now have a refined picture of the public. Americans are not so "fed up" or "angry" with press freedoms as conventional wisdom would have us believe. Certainly there has been little love lost between the public as a whole and the sensationalist press organizations and news outlets that act irresponsibly. Yet that outrage has not translated into calls for regulating news organizations as a whole. Nor has it translated into support for applying restrictions to those news organizations and media outlets whose harms seem most apparent – a group that would include the *National Enquirer*, *Hustler* magazine, and "The Jerry Springer Show" among its ranks. The reservoir of good will toward the freedom of the press is not drained simply because particular outlets provoke dismay or disgust. Rather, the public lends its support to press freedoms across the board, qualified only by societal concerns of invasiveness and easy accessibility.

In 1966, V. O. Key Jr. admonished in *The Responsible Electorate* that the "perverse and unorthodox argument of this little book is that voters are not fools" (Key, 1966: 7). His message inspired a reconsideration of the abilities of the public and its capacities for democratic governance. Strong empirical work by Page and Shapiro (1992) and many others have debunked the centuries-old myth that citizens are irrational, given to emotional whims, and unworthy of democracy. Our work similarly demonstrates that the public does indeed think coherently and rationally about free press rights – their value in democratic society and how they ought to be applied. Thanks to Key, today we may advance the not-so-perverse and rather orthodox view that citizens are not fools.

7

Public Opinion, the First Amendment, and the Challenges of the Twenty-First Century

James Madison's experience with the Virginia Bill of Rights was by no means reassuring: Its provisions had been flagrantly ignored whenever they were "opposed to a popular current." Thus Madison openly doubted whether adding an explicit bill of rights to a federal constitution built on the premise of enumerated powers would perform much of a service, especially during those moments when its guarantees were most controversial. Notwithstanding the explicit provisions contained in the Bill of Rights that was ratified in 1791, Madison firmly believed that continued public support for those provisions would also be required, lest they be reduced to mere "parchment barriers" against legislative or executive tyranny.

Throughout this book we have taken Madison's fears to heart in exploring the relationship between public opinion and freedom of the press. We examined public knowledge of freedom of the press at the broad level of its existence in the U.S. Constitution, and we investigated public awareness of freedom of the press issues as they apply to contemporary U.S. society. We explored dimensions of support for freedom of the press and attempted to come to grips with "abstract" and "specific" conceptualizations of it. And we studied the approach the public takes to applying press freedoms in a rather complex media environment – one filled with a variety of different forms of media (ranging from the Internet to newspapers to television) as well as very different sources within each medium (ranging from *Hustler* and "The Jerry Springer Show" to *Business Week* and "NBC Nightly News"). In addressing these issues, we attempted to demonstrate the theoretical significance of the relationship between public opinion and freedom of the press. The thrust of our findings is that the public's orientation toward freedom of the press remains remarkably positive, despite a poorly performing media. We thus conclude that Madison's fears of the "popular current" have been allayed, at least for the time being.

In this chapter we summarize the key findings from our study and discuss their implications for the future. First, we review the main points articulated in the previous chapters, then we apply what we have learned to the systems theory and rational public frameworks offered by previous scholars, and finally we discuss the challenges that lie ahead for the freedom of the press as the United States embarks on its twenty-first-century course.

CONTEMPORARY PUBLIC OPINION AND THE FREEDOM OF THE PRESS

At the turn of the twenty-first century, we find an American public that strongly values the rights of the free press. While confidence in the modern-day news media has fallen to an all-time low, Americans remain steadfast in their affinity for the goals engrained in the First Amendment's protection of the press.

Public reaction to press coverage of a number of major events (including the O. J. Simpson trial, the death of Princess Diana, and the Clinton-Lewinsky scandal), however, has been almost universally negative, adding fuel to the already wavering confidence that Americans maintain in the media. Whereas in the early 1970s some polls showed that confidence in the news media had risen to as high as 68 percent, by the late 1990s that figure had dipped significantly. Other polls show that confidence in journalism has dropped from 50 percent to 25 percent over the past decade. Scholars have attributed these declines to public distaste for numerous newsgathering practices, the negative orientation of news, and the willingness of the media to delve into the personal lives of public officials (and other high-visibility individuals) and give disproportionately large coverage to certain stories, among other factors.

At the same time, Americans remain committed to First Amendment freedoms and to the freedom of the press in particular. For example, we found that nearly nineteen out of twenty Americans say that if there were a public vote on the First Amendment today, they would vote to ratify it once again, and two-thirds of the public disagrees with the notion that the First Amendment has gone too far in the rights it guarantees. And when asked if news organizations should be allowed to report or publicize what they think is appropriate to report, fully two-thirds of the public supports these abstract press rights.

To be sure, some of our data offer cautionary advice regarding public opinion for freedom of the press. From 1997 to 1999, we measured a 15-percentage-point decline in those who said the contemporary press had either "the right amount of" or "too little" freedom. In 1999, fully half of the public said that the press has "too much freedom." So while public support for press rights remains strong, contemporary dissatisfaction with the news media's performance, particularly in their coverage of "big" stories such as Clinton-Lewinsky, may be eating away at the glue that bonds the public to the values of a free and unfettered press.

Stouffer (1955), McCloskey and Brill (1983), and Prothro and Grigg (1960) all argued that Americans tend to be enormously supportive of abstract freedoms, but when it comes to specific, potentially controversial circumstances, that same public tends to forgo such principles and tolerate government denials of freedom to those with whom the public disagrees. Certainly, large-scale mass support for abstract rights under the broad construct of "the freedom of the press" continues today. Yet in numerous instances, there is also strong support for specific conditions in which the press might choose to exercise its rights. Specifically, we found that eight in ten Americans believe that journalists should be allowed to keep their news sources confidential, about three-quarters think that broadcasters should be allowed to televise both courtroom trials and the proceedings of the U.S. Supreme Court, two-thirds support the right of newspapers to publish with no prior restraint, and more than six in ten support the right of newspapers to endorse and criticize political candidates.

However, there do remain some important concrete circumstances in which less than a majority of Americans supports free press activities. These include support for the news media to publish government secrets (48 percent), to use hidden cameras as a newsgathering practice (27 percent), and to project winners of an election while people are still voting (29 percent). In line with Supreme Court decisions on the subject, the public is also largely unwilling to allow high school students to report on controversial material in school newspapers without the approval of school officials (37 percent). Finally, negative public reactions to the way in which the news media have reported on public figures in recent times led only 38 percent of Americans to support the idea that journalists should be allowed to investigate the private lives of public people. These figures point to acceptance of the "qualification hypothesis" – the public is apparently defining the freedom of the press in such a way that those few examples fall outside the bounds of the freedom itself.

In addition to exploring public support for freedom of the press at the abstract and concrete levels, this book also examined knowledge and awareness of free expression and free press in particular. We found that about half of the adult public claims to have had at least one course in either school or college that dealt with First Amendment issues. On the educational system's performance in delivering instruction on First Amendment issues, about six in ten Americans offer less-than-enthusiastic evaluations. Still, the majority of Americans report that they pay at least some attention to First Amendment issues, and about half are able to express concretely some knowledge of First Amendment topics that are under debate. Americans are also quite willing to admit that they too often take for granted the free expression rights guaranteed by the First Amendment.

Perhaps it is the lack of salience of important First Amendment rights, such as freedom of the press, that leads many to feel that these rights are taken for granted. Our surveys find that only about one in ten members of the general public is able to identify freedom of the press as a right that is in the First Amendment, even though about half are able to place freedom of speech on that list. Freedom to practice religion and the right to bear arms both are more frequently mentioned as "important" constitutional rights than is freedom of the press. Four in ten Americans cannot name any specific rights in the First Amendment.

Knowledge and awareness of free press rights is important to a healthy democracy. In many cases, knowledge encourages the full exercise of those rights, which in turn facilitates the flow of ideas and information, thus fortifying the free marketplace of ideas. Our study indicates that while many in the public are aware and knowledgeable, there is clearly room for improvement – particularly in the domain of freedom of the press issues. Lack of attention to free expression issues in the educational system and poor ratings of the educational system's delivery of instruction on free expression may indicate that broad curricular improvements will enhance awareness and knowledge of these important rights.

Finally, our study sheds light on how the public contrasts different forms of media in terms of those press rights that they are willing to extend. We examined differences across the following types of media: the Internet, magazines, broadcast television, basic cable television, premium subscription cable television, and radio. We also tested the public's limits of free press rights for billboards and video stores. Using the publication of "sexually explicit material" as the controlled content, we found that the public makes significant distinctions across these various media in the free press rights it is willing to extend.

Both accessibility of the medium and its invasive nature appear to be the key criteria used to distinguish among the media in the public's willingness to extend press rights. A video store rental – because of its more restricted access and the fact that it requires more active acquisition of the material – is the medium to which the public is most likely to extend press rights. Specifically, 63 percent agree that people should be allowed to rent sexually explicit videos from video stores. A similarly high (59 percent) number of Americans are willing to extend this right to premium subscription cable television channels. Again, with subscription cable TV, access is relatively more controlled and passive exposure is far less likely to occur. Fewer people (44 percent) agree that magazines should be extended the right to publish sexually explicit material. Magazines must be purchased, and so access is somewhat limited. However, the likelihood of passive exposure to a magazine on display at a newsstand or other store is greater than the likelihood of unwanted exposure to a subscription cable broadcast.

By contrast, support for press freedoms drops considerably for the remaining media that we tested. For radio, the Internet, and basic cable television, only about one-quarter to one-third of the public agreed that individuals should be able to get sexually explicit material from these media. Radio offers words and no pictures but is readily accessible to most individuals; basic cable TV is more readily accessible – as most American homes have it – than premium channels; and Internet access is broad, particularly for younger people. Passive exposure to material on these three media is greater than for premium cable, video store rentals, and magazines.

Public support for allowing sexually explicit material on broadcast TV and on billboards is also very low (18 percent and 9 percent, respectively). The significant opportunities for being passively exposed to material on these media, along with the ease of access to them, lead most in the general public to tolerate restrictions on press rights with regard to these particular media, at least as far as their publishing sexually explicit material is concerned.

Based on the criteria of "invasiveness" and "accessibility," the public appears to distinguish between different forms of media in its willingness to allow press rights. But there are significant demographic differences in public willingness to extend press rights. Across all media forms, men are more likely to agree that sexually explicit material should be allowed. The gender gap may be the result of the specific sexual nature of the material we used to test: Women may be more offended than men by the content of what we tested. Also, younger people tended to be more willing to extend rights, across all media, for allowing sexually explicit material. Again, this may not be so surprising, given generational differences in sensitivity to sexual mores.

More substantively interesting are the differences by level of knowledge and by level of education in public willingness to extend press rights. Those who are more knowledgeable about the First Amendment and those with higher levels of education are more likely to support the right of the press to publish sexually explicit material across the various forms of media. Education and knowledge appear to have a significant impact on support for press rights. These findings further suggest that improvements in the educational system's ability to incorporate First Amendment instruction are likely to enhance the integrity of those rights in our society. In short, the more people know about and think about First Amendment issues, the more appreciative they become of them and the more willing they are to support them under conditions that they may find personally objectionable.

A final overall finding is perhaps the most significant one, and it certainly reinforces the argument that the public's approach to applying free press protections is "rational" and less subject to emotional reactions to content or to the "popular current." This finding relates to the public's willingness to extend the similar protections of press rights to very different media sources that are *within* the same medium. When our respondents were asked to compare tabloid newspapers with elite newspapers, serious news magazines with magazines that are sexually explicit in nature, and traditional television news programs with sensationalistic television talk shows, most were willing to extend the same rights to all sources within a particular medium. For example, more than seven in ten said that tabloid newspapers such as the *Star* and the *National Enquirer* should have the same freedom to publish what they want as the *New York Times* and the *Wall Street Journal.* Seven in ten also said that magazines like *Playboy* and *Hustler* should have the same publishing freedoms as *Time* and *Newsweek*, and six in ten extended to Jerry Springer and Jenny Jones the same rights that are given to "ABC News with Peter Jennings."

In the aggregate, the public once again displays a sophisticated "content neutral" approach to extending press freedoms for various specific news sources within a particular medium. The nature of the material appears to be less of a factor than the format in which the material is presented. Most believe that news organizations of varying reputation and prestige should be afforded the same rights, provided that those organizations present material through the same medium. Once again, the public appears to be more sophisticated; its approach is similar to the one the courts have used in applying free press principles. This sophistication – apparent in varying degrees throughout this book – should give supporters of free press rights confidence as they weather a period in U.S. history characterized by considerable public dissatisfaction with the performance of the Fourth Estate.

INTERPRETING PUBLIC SUPPORT FOR PRESS FREEDOMS

David Easton's systems theory provided us with an initial framework by which we could view and assess the nature of public support for key individual rights, including the freedom of the press. Our main purpose, however, was to seek more insight into the nature of "the rational public," a term that has been central to a number of recent works on public opinion. Is the public so rational when it comes to the highly charged and controversial question of whether constitutional rights should be extended to society's least popular groups?

Add the media of today to that list of traditional American pariahs who, perhaps because they garner little sympathy from the American public, are most interested in exercising their theoretical rights under the Constitution. As our 1997 and 1999 studies make clear, a majority of Americans do express feelings of "trust, confidence, or affection," although not toward members of the press. Rather, their confidence and trust lie with the freedoms that the press relies upon. This distinction is of course a crucial aspect of our findings. Recall that at the outset, we cited the fears of recent scholars, who warned us that any significant reduction in support for particular institutions, actors, or sets of events might drain the public's more general support for the underlying system and the set of rules governing the system. In the immediate context, those fears seem unfounded. Critical drops in support for members of the press and press institutions have not led to reduced public support for a core principle underlying the U.S. system: the First Amendment guarantee of freedom of the press.

Systems theory provides a useful framework in this narrow respect: Easton posited that while levels of support for actors are expected to ebb and flow to varying degrees, we should concern ourselves primarily with reductions in overall support for the system and its rules. By drawing such a clear distinction, Easton helps us keep an eye on the more important targets of concern.

Sanford, Richards, and others feared that unfortunate and controversial events might cause such precipitous drops in specific support that they could drain the citizens' reservoir of good will toward the political system as a whole. In short, they believe the bridge from distrust of the press to distrust of press rights may have already been crossed. Yet as the 1997 and 1999 data make clear, that bridge has *not* yet been crossed. Certainly much of the anecdotal and empirical evidence reveals a trend toward public distrust and a growing lack of confidence in the press itself. Yet so far, the public's desire to "shoot the messenger" has not translated into a drop in overall support for press freedoms. Although the messenger itself has been tainted, public support for its right to deliver messages remains virtually unaffected. To be sure, polarizing events such as the Clinton-Lewinsky affair have directed public attention (and in many cases scorn) at particular aspects of press coverage. Thus, for example, the public was considerably less supportive of press efforts to reveal the private lives of officials in 1999; this was unmistakably part of the fallout from the Clinton impeachment scandal. But even more remarkable is the degree to which that fallout in public support has been contained, at least with respect to press freedoms. Even after a full year of the Clinton-Lewinsky event's near-daily bombardment of the reservoir of good will, the public remained unwilling to curtail press freedoms unrelated to the Clinton-Lewinsky scandal, and its support for the freedom of the press in general remained strong indeed. Calls for censorship and government regulation of the press continue to fall on deaf ears among the masses. The reservoir of good will for press freedoms apparently has a lot left in its reserves.

The public's mature and quite thoughtful approach to press freedoms parallels the rational approach it has taken elsewhere, as documented by Page and Shapiro and others. The public has not allowed its own lack of confidence in members of the press and press institutions to compromise the legitimacy of the U.S. political system. In that respect, the public has proven itself to be a remarkably sophisticated consumer of news and information.

While our findings bode well for the continued exercise of free press in the United States, they should nevertheless give pause to those in the press who may push the limits of this public trust. Public distaste for the press has become so intense and pervasive that if it is not eventually treated, it could become a deadly cancer on the political system. The good will of the public is not a bottomless well. If public confidence in the press continues to decline at its current pace, the press could become so disliked that it would become impossible for even the most sophisticated members of the public to distinguish between members of the press on one hand and the goals they are striving to achieve on the other. At that point, calls for government censorship and reduced discretion to publish might well garner significant popular support. The power of negative association should not be underestimated in this context. Members of the press are essentially the public representatives of the freedom of the press, and their apparent reluctance to go the extra mile to restore the public trust may one day take its toll.

Fortunately, there are signs that the press understands it is on an increasingly short leash with the American public. Upon hearing of a possible twenty-year-old sexual assault by then-Governor Bill Clinton, NBC sat on the explosive story for weeks while it searched for some corroborating evidence that the accusations (made by Juanita Broaddrick) were accurate. (NBC News ultimately did run the story, but only after heated disagreements within the news division were resolved in its favor.) Fox News quickly parted ways with its correspondent Matt Drudge when he insisted on displaying a potentially inflammatory photograph of an aborted fetus on one newscast. Of course such displays of journalistic caution are not a brand-new phenomenon; but in light of the exceedingly low image of the current press, they now garner disproportionate attention. Whether they can begin to shift public perceptions of the press is another matter entirely. But it is a critical matter indeed if the press plans to continue basking in the public's support for press freedoms.

FUTURE IMPLICATIONS FOR THE FREEDOM OF THE PRESS

The overriding message of this book is one of guarded optimism. The reservoir of good will toward the freedom of the press continues to hold, even though the profession that relies on this reservoir is held in exceedingly low regard by the public. The United States' tradition of a robust press apparently holds greater weight with the American public than most of its members care to admit. Other constitutional rights, such as freedom of speech or of religion, routinely garner higher abstract support numbers, but press freedoms do not lag far behind. And public support for press freedoms is as deep as it is wide: Despite bombardment after bombardment in recent years, press freedoms remain popular with the public. Terms such as "censorship" and "advance government approval" do not drum up much interest; in fact, the media employ such hyperbole to *increase support* for their own press activities. "The Jerry Springer Show" and the *National Enquirer* are as much a beneficiary of this good will as their more respected colleagues in the industry. Although the press has become an institution that the American public loves to hate, restrictions on the press are considered the greater evil by far.

Still, if the picture we present is an overall positive one for supporters of a free press, some dangers still lurk on the horizon. Perhaps the single most important technological development in the United States during the past decade has been the growth of the personal computer industry. The proliferation of computers for a variety of personal and professional uses has changed numerous aspects of daily life. So-called "e-commerce" has become the next great business frontier, with millions of consumers rushing to purchase all varieties of consumer goods over the Internet. Politicians campaign for votes through the use of innovative campaign Web sites, and they increasingly measure public moods by Internet polling. Thanks to the computer and the Internet, more information is now available to the public than ever before.

For the press, this new age of the Internet carries with it some potential pitfalls. When the press adheres to its central function in a democratic system – to educate the masses, disseminate information, and facilitate public debate – the Internet can further these goals in numerous ways. Because World Wide Web sites may be viewed by anyone with access to the Internet, local newspapers can reach audiences that were previously out of reach. Newspapers and magazines – formerly limited to those who lived along U.S. Postal Service and newspaper carrier routes – can now reach anyone with a phone line. News grows stale more quickly as well. In the past, newspapers and magazines could not compete with radio and television to provide breaking news. Today they stand on near-equal footing, with newspapers' Web sites weighing in on events almost immediately. Consumers can respond directly to writers and publishers of this information, creating an interactive dialogue that educates both sides. Finally, traditional considerations of space – fueled by printing and broadcast costs – don't apply to the world of the Internet. The "marketplace of ideas" has become a fast and furious place indeed, with nearly unlimited potential to transmit information and ideas and to foster public awareness and debate.

But along with these advantages comes the temptation on the part of the press to move ever faster and ever more furiously to stake its claim in the marketplace. As was noted in Chapter 1, those who write stories or produce information for Internet Web sites do not work within "deadlines," as that term has traditionally been understood. Publication on the Internet can take place at any time, shrinking the window of opportunity that print reporters normally enjoy to check sources and verify information. While radio and television news outlets have always felt pressure to rush "breaking news" onto the air, print reporters don't usually work under such conditions. The results of this new rush online have not always been positive. For example, *Newsweek*'s traditional weekly deadline was rendered irrelevant during the early days of its Clinton-Lewinsky coverage; instead of verifying its story for publication in its weekly magazine, the pressure to outmaneuver the competition led it to prematurely reveal details of the affair on its Web site. Because news and information are disseminated so much faster on the Internet, inaccurate reports can quickly root themselves in the public consciousness.

An equally important facet of the new computer age is the expansion of the term "press" to include anyone who uses his or her home computer to disseminate news and information. The rise of the "desktop publisher" is a development that has not been ignored either by the mainstream media or by the political institutions of government. Matt Drudge parlayed his personal Web site into one of the most frequently visited sites on the Internet, and then later into a short-lived correspondent's job on Fox News. The Internet magazine *Salon* was the first to report that Henry Hyde – the lead House manager in the Senate impeachment trial of President Bill Clinton – may have had an adulterous affair in his past. (The president's defenders claimed that this smacked of hypocrisy; others argued that the two situations were not analogous.) White House and Congressional offices routinely canvass individual Web sites and chat rooms, both to gauge the public mood and to identify targets of future public relations campaigns. Most interest groups actively maintain their own Web sites, allowing them to participate in political dialogues by disseminating information and evidence that support their positions. These often elaborate Web sites are generally cheaper to produce than direct-mail campaigns or television ads and can reach far greater segments of the population than a flier or newsletter. Even the ability to send e-mails to large numbers of strangers is itself a form of publication by most definitions. The freedom of the press now encompasses a much greater variety of media than ever before and may be exercised by almost anyone.

A number of questions must be left for future study: Will the continued proliferation of Internet publishers transform the essential meaning of the "freedom of the press," both in the courts and in the arena of public opinion? Will public support for press freedoms erode once we come to automatically associate that freedom with the right of nearly anyone to publish almost anything at any time? Certainly that possibility exists. Or perhaps this First Amendment freedom will become even more cherished once it is viewed as a right that nearly everyone exercises. For the first 200 years of U.S. history, the public understood the freedom of the press to be a right exercised by a few, for the benefit (it was hoped) of many. Altering that equation significantly – it is now becoming a right exercised by many, for the benefit of many – will entail some growing pains. So far the regime has survived these developments quite admirably. Whether it will continue to do so remains to be seen. But the continued legitimacy of the political system requires nothing less.

Appendix: Annotated Questionnaires

Hello, my name is _____ and I am calling from the University of Connecticut. We are conducting a survey on important issues facing the nation. To determine who in your household I need to speak with, could you please tell me which person in your household age 18 or older has had the most recent birthday? (If not respondent ask to speak with him or her.)

1. As you know the U.S. Constitution provides citizens many rights and freedoms. Are there any particular rights or freedoms that you feel are most important to American society? (PROBE: Are there any others you can name?)

1997	1999	
5%	6%	Freedom of the press
50	50	Freedom of speech
5	5	Freedom not to practice religion
14	13	Freedom to practice religion
1	2	Right to petition
4	4	Right of assembly/Right of association
9	14	Right to bear arms/or guns
2	3	Right to trial by jury/Fair trial
1	3	Right to privacy
1	1	Freedom from unreasonable search
–	1	Right to protest
–	6	Right to vote
11	14	Other
30	24	DK/Ref

2. As you may know, the First Amendment is part of the U.S. Constitution. Can you name any of the specific rights that are guaranteed by the First Amendment? (PROBE: Are there any others you can name?)

1997	1999	
11%	12%	Freedom of the press
49	44	Freedom of speech

21	13	Freedom of religion
2	2	Right to petition
10	8	Right of assembly/association
7	6	Other
37	49	DK/Ref

3. The U.S. Constitution protects certain rights, but not everyone considers each right important. I am going to read you some rights guaranteed by the U.S. Constitution. Please tell me how important it is that you have that right. First, how important is the (ROTATE ITEMS BELOW). . . . Is it essential that you have that right, important but not essential, or not that important? [All figures are from 1997.]

	Essential	Important	Not important	DK
a. You have the right to assemble, march, protest, or petition the government	56%	36%	7%	1%
b. You have the right to speak freely about whatever you want	72	27	1	–
c. You have the right to practice the religion of your choice	81	18	1	–
d. You have the right to practice no religion	66	24	9	1
e. You have the right to be informed by a free press	60	33	6	1
f. You have the right to own firearms	33	31	33	3
g. You have the right to privacy	78	21	1	–
h. You have the right to a fair trial	86	14	–	–

4. The First Amendment became part of the U.S. Constitution more than 200 years ago. This is what it says: "Congress shall make no law respecting an establishment of religion or prohibiting the free exercise thereof, or of abridging the freedom of speech or of the press, or the right of the people peaceably to assemble, and to petition the government for a redress of grievances." Imagine that the country were again voting to ratify the First Amendment. If you were voting on whether or not to approve it, how would you vote?

1997

93%	Approve
4	Not approve
3	DK/Ref

5. The First Amendment became part of the U.S. Constitution more than 200 years ago. This is what it says: "Congress shall make no law respecting an establishment of religion or prohibiting the free exercise thereof, or of abridging the freedom of speech or of the press, or the right of the people peaceably to assemble, and to petition the government for a redress of grievances." Based on your own feelings about the First Amendment, please tell me whether you agree or disagree with the following statement: The First Amendment goes too far in the rights it guarantees.

1999

16%	Strongly agree
12	Mildly agree
22	Mildly disagree
45	Strongly disagree
5	DK/Ref

6. How closely do you pay attention to issues involving the First Amendment's freedoms of speech, press, religion, assembly, and petition – do you pay a lot of attention, some, just a little, or not much at all?

1997

39%	A lot
45	Some
9	A little
6	Not much
–	DK/Ref

7. Please tell me if you agree or disagree with the following statement: Americans don't appreciate First Amendment freedoms the way they ought to. PROBE: Do you strongly or mildly (agree/disagree)?

1997

47%	Strongly agree
29	Mildly agree
12	Mildly disagree
8	Strongly disagree
4	DK/Ref

8. Are the rights guaranteed by the First Amendment something you personally think about or are they something you take for granted?

1999

42%	Personally think about
54	Take for granted
3	DK/Ref

9. What about most people in the United States – do you think the rights guaranteed by the First Amendment are something people specifically think about or are they something they take for granted?

1999

9%	Personally think about
87	Take for granted
4	DK/Ref

10. Even though the U.S. Constitution guarantees freedom of the press, government has placed some restrictions on it. Overall, do you think the press in America has too much freedom to do what it wants, too little freedom to do what it wants, or is the amount of freedom the press has about right?

1997	1999	
38%	53%	Too much freedom
9	7	Too little freedom
50	37	About right
3	2	DK/Ref

11. Even though the U.S. Constitution guarantees freedom of speech, government has placed some restrictions on it. Overall, do you think Americans have too much freedom to speak freely, too little freedom to speak freely, or is the amount of freedom people have to speak freely about right?

1997	1999	
10%	12%	Too much freedom
18	26	Too little freedom
68	59	About right
4	3	DK/Ref

12. Even though the U.S. Constitution guarantees freedom of religion, government has placed some restrictions on it. Overall, do you think Americans have too much religious freedom, too little religious freedom, or is the amount of religious freedom people have about right?

1997	1999	
6%	8%	Too much freedom
21	26	Too little freedom
71	63	About right
2	3	DK/Ref

13. Do you think that imposing curfews on young people violates their First Amendment rights or not?

1997	1999	
19%	18%	Violates rights
78	78	Does not violate rights
3	4	DK/Ref

14. Now I'm going to read a series of statements about how people might try to exercise their rights under the First Amendment. Please tell me whether you think under current law Americans have the legal right or not to do the following (RANDOMIZE Q a–f):

a. Under current law, do Americans have the legal right to burn the American flag as a means of political protest? Yes or no?

1999	
33%	Yes
64	No
3	DK/Ref

b. Under current law, do the courts have the right to send reporters to jail for refusing to reveal a news source? Yes or no?

1999
37%	Yes
54	No
9	DK/Ref

c. Under current law, does the government have the right to restrict indecent material on the Internet? Yes or no?

1999
53%	Yes
40	No
7	DK/Ref

d. Under current law, do controversial groups that hold unpopular beliefs have the legal right to demonstrate peacefully in public? Yes or no?

1999
86%	Yes
12	No
2	DK/Ref

e. Under current law, does a science teacher in a public school have the legal right to teach the Biblical view of creation as an alternative to Darwin's theory of evolution in class? Yes or no?

1999
42%	Yes
50	No
8	DK/Ref

f. Under current law, does someone have the legal right to shout "Fire" in a crowded arena as a prank? Yes or no?

1999
7%	Yes
91	No
2	DK/Ref

15. To the best of your recollection, have you ever taken classes in either school or college that dealt with the First Amendment?

1999
52%	Yes
47	No
2	DK/Ref

16. Would that have been grade school, high school, college, or somewhere else?

1999
5%	Grade school
63	High school
29	College

2   Somewhere else
–   DK/Ref

17. Overall, how would you rate the job that the American educational system is doing in teaching students about First Amendment freedoms – excellent, good, only fair, or poor?

1997
4%   Excellent
26   Good
41   Only fair
22   Poor
6   DK/Ref

18. Please tell me whether or not you have done any of the following in the past year. (ROTATE ITEMS a–f.)

a. Displayed an American flag

1997	**1999**	
62%	56%	Yes
38	44	No
–	–	DK/Ref

b. Signed a petition

1999	
54%	Yes
45	No
1	DK/Ref

c. Voted in an election

1997	**1999**	
80%	73%	Yes
20	27	No
–	–	DK/Ref

d. Participated in a political rally

1997	**1999**	
14%	10%	Yes
86	90	No
–	–	DK/Ref

e. Attended a public meeting

1997	**1999**	
58%	50%	Yes
42	49	No
–	–	DK/Ref

f. Contacted an elected official

1997	**1999**	
43%	38%	Yes
57	62	No
–	–	DK/Ref

g. Sent a letter to the editor

1997	1999	
12%	12%	Yes
88	88	No
–	–	DK/Ref

19. Please tell me if you agree or disagree with the following statement: People should be allowed to express their opinion, whatever that may be.

1999	
64%	Strongly agree
26	Mildly agree
6	Mildly disagree
3	Strongly disagree
1	DK/Ref

I am going to read you some ways people might exercise their First Amendment right of free speech. For each, tell me if you agree or disagree that someone should be allowed to do it.

a. Companies should be allowed to advertise tobacco.

1997	1999	
26%	32%	Strongly agree
30	39	Mildly agree
11	8	Mildly disagree
31	20	Strongly disagree
3	1	DK/Ref

b. Companies should be allowed to advertise tobacco on TV.

1999	
24%	Strongly agree
27	Mildly agree
10	Mildly disagree
37	Strongly disagree
1	DK/Ref

c. Companies should be allowed to advertise liquor and alcohol products.

1997	1999	
25%	24%	Strongly agree
35	39	Mildly agree
12	7	Mildly disagree
26	29	Strongly disagree
2	–	DK/Ref

d. Companies should be allowed to advertise liquor and alcohol products on TV.

1999	
24%	Strongly agree
27	Mildly agree
10	Mildly disagree

38   Strongly disagree
1   DK/Ref

e. The media should be allowed to broadcast pictures of nude or partially clothed persons.

1997	1999	
8%	5%	Strongly agree
19	16	Mildly agree
19	15	Mildly disagree
52	62	Strongly disagree
3	1	DK/Ref

f. People should be allowed to express unpopular opinions.

1997	1999	
68%	58%	Strongly agree
22	28	Mildly agree
5	8	Mildly disagree
4	5	Strongly disagree
1	1	DK/Ref

g. Companies should be allowed to advertise tobacco on billboards.

1999	
28%	Strongly agree
35	Mildly agree
8	Mildly disagree
28	Strongly disagree
1	DK/Ref

h. Companies should be allowed to advertise liquor and alcohol products on billboards.

1999	
25%	Strongly agree
35	Mildly agree
11	Mildly disagree
29	Strongly disagree
–	DK/Ref

i. Musicians should be allowed to sing songs with words that others might find offensive.

1997	1999	
23%	27%	Strongly agree
28	29	Mildly agree
16	15	Mildly disagree
31	26	Strongly disagree
3	4	DK/Ref

j. People should be allowed to place sexually explicit material on the Internet.

1997	1999	
10%	10%	Strongly agree
15	14	Mildly agree
10	12	Mildly disagree
62	63	Strongly disagree
3	1	DK/Ref

k. People should be allowed to burn or deface the American flag as a political statement.

1997	1999	
10%	10%	Strongly agree
10	10	Mildly agree
8	6	Mildly disagree
70	74	Strongly disagree
2	1	DK/Ref

l. School students should be allowed to wear a t-shirt with a message or picture that others may find offensive.

1997	1999	
9%	10%	Strongly agree
17	17	Mildly agree
22	23	Mildly disagree
48	48	Strongly disagree
4	2	DK/Ref

m. People should be allowed to use words in public that might be offensive to racial groups.

1997	1999	
8%	8%	Strongly agree
15	13	Mildly agree
14	16	Mildly disagree
61	62	Strongly disagree
2	1	DK/Ref

n. People should be allowed to display in a public place art that has content that might be offensive to others.

1997	1999	
20%	17%	Strongly agree
24	24	Mildly agree
22	24	Mildly disagree
31	33	Strongly disagree
4	2	DK/Ref

20. Some people feel that the U.S. Constitution should be amended to make it illegal to burn or desecrate the American flag as a form of political dissent. Others say that the U.S. Constitution should not be amended to specifically prohibit flag burning. Do you think the U.S. Constitution should or should not be amended to prohibit burning or desecrating the flag?

1997

49%	Should be amended
49	Should not be amended
2	DK/Ref

IF "SHOULD BE" ASK:

a. If an amendment prohibiting flag burning were approved, it would be the first time any of the freedoms in the First Amendment has been amended in over 200 years. Knowing this, would you still support an amendment to prohibit flag burning?

1997

88%	Yes
9	No
3	DK/Ref

21. Please tell me if you agree or disagree with the following statement: It's dangerous to restrict freedom of speech because restricting the freedom of one person could lead to restrictions on everbody. PROBE: Do you strongly or mildly (agree/disagree)?

1997

59%	Strongly agree
24	Mildly agree
8	Mildly disagree
6	Strongly disagree
3	DK/Ref

22. Recently a federal jury ruled that a Web site featuring "wanted" posters listing abortion doctors' names and addresses amounted to death threats and therefore ordered the site's authors to pay damages. How much have you heard about this? A lot, some, a little, or none?

1999

11%	A lot
21	Some
24	A little
44	None
–	DK/Ref

23. Do you think this ruling is or is not a violation of the sites authors' First Amendment rights?

1999

43%	Is
41	Is not
16	DK/Ref

24. Tell me if you agree or disagree with the following statement: News organizations should be allowed to report or publish what they think is appropriate to report.

1999

31%	Strongly agree
35	Mildly agree
14	Mildly disagree
16	Strongly disagree
4	DK/Ref

25. I'm going to read you some ways that freedom of the press may be exercised. For each, tell me if you agree or disagree that the press should be allowed to do it.

   a. Newspapers should be allowed to publish freely without government approval of a story.

1997	**1999**	
56%	38%	Strongly agree
24	27	Mildly agree
11	14	Mildly disagree
6	18	Strongly disagree
3	3	DK/Ref

   b. Journalists should be allowed to keep a news source confidential.

1997	**1999**	
58%	48%	Strongly agree
27	31	Mildly agree
6	10	Mildly disagree
6	9	Strongly disagree
2	3	DK/Ref

   c. Broadcasters should be allowed to televise courtroom trials.

1997	**1999**	
28%	34%	Strongly agree
23	33	Mildly agree
19	13	Mildly disagree
25	17	Strongly disagree
4	3	DK/Ref

   d. Newspapers should be allowed to endorse or criticize political candidates.

1997	**1999**	
43%	35%	Strongly agree
26	28	Mildly agree
11	14	Mildly disagree
18	22	Strongly disagree
2	2	DK/Ref

   e. The news media should be allowed to report government secrets that have come to journalists' attention.

1997	1999	
35%	23%	Strongly agree
26	25	Mildly agree
14	18	Mildly disagree
21	30	Strongly disagree
5	3	DK/Ref

f. Television networks should be allowed to project winners of an election while people are still voting.

1997	1999	
15%	11%	Strongly agree
16	18	Mildly agree
17	19	Mildly disagree
51	51	Strongly disagree
1	1	DK/Ref

g. High school students should be allowed to report controversial issues in their student newspapers without the approval of school authorities.

1997	1999	
24%	19%	Strongly agree
21	18	Mildly agree
23	27	Mildly disagree
29	33	Strongly disagree
3	3	DK/Ref

h. Journalists should be allowed to use hidden cameras in their reporting.

1997	1999	
13%	9%	Strongly agree
18	18	Mildly agree
20	18	Mildly disagree
45	54	Strongly disagree
3	1	DK/Ref

i. Broadcasters should be allowed to televise the proceedings of the U.S. Supreme Court.

1999	
44%	Strongly agree
29	Mildly agree
11	Mildly disagree
12	Strongly disagree
3	DK/Ref

j. Journalists should be allowed to investigate the private lives of public figures.

1999	
17%	Strongly agree
21	Mildly agree
18	Mildly disagree

42	Strongly disagree
1	DK/Ref

26. Do you agree or disagree with the following statement? Any group that wants to should be allowed to hold a rally for a cause or issue even if it may be offensive to others in the community.

1997	**1999**	
38%	30%	Strongly agree
34	32	Mildly agree
10	16	Mildly disagree
15	20	Strongly disagree
3	3	DK/Ref

27. Do you agree or disagree with the following statement? The government should regulate what appears on television.

1999	
20%	Strongly agree
25	Mildly agree
21	Mildly disagree
32	Strongly disagree
2	DK/Ref

28. As you may know, most public libraries have computers that visitors may use to access information on the Internet. I'm going to read you two statements. Please tell me which one comes closest to your own opinion. Some people think (READ FIRST CHOICE). Other people think (READ SECOND CHOICE). Which of these comes closest to your own opinion?)

1999	
58%	that public libraries should block access to certain Internet sites that might offend some people
38	that public library users should have access to all Internet sites
4	DK/Ref

29. People get their news and information from many different sources. What do you consider to be your primary source for the news? Newspapers, television, radio, magazines, the Internet, or some other source?

1999	
25%	Newspaper
56	Television
11	Radio
1	Magazines
3	Internet
2	Other (specify)
1	DK/Ref

30. To the best of your recollection, have you read or heard anything about a recent U.S. Supreme Court ruling regarding the Internet? IF YES: How much have you heard – a lot, some, or just a little?

1997

49%	Read/heard nothing
8	A lot
19	Some
22	A little
1	DK/Ref

31. As you may know, courts have traditionally given broad First Amendment protections to books and newspapers containing material that may be offensive to some people. Recently the U.S. Supreme Court ruled that material on the Internet has the same First Amendment protections as printed material such as books and newspapers. Do you agree or disagree with this ruling – strongly or mildly?

1997	**1999**	
30%	31%	Strongly agree
26	33	Mildly agree
15	17	Mildly disagree
23	14	Strongly disagree
5	6	DK/Ref

32. I'm going to read you some ways people might exercise their First Amendment right of free speech. For each, tell me if you agree or disagree that someone should be allowed to do it.

a. People should be allowed to place sexually explicit material on the Internet.

1997	**1999**	
10%	11%	Strongly agree
15	19	Mildly agree
10	13	Mildly disagree
62	55	Strongly disagree
3	2	DK/Ref

b. People should be allowed to publish sexually explicit material in magazines.

1999	
16%	Strongly agree
29	Mildly agree
12	Mildly disagree
41	Strongly disagree
1	DK/Ref

c. Broadcast television, such as networks like NBC and CBS, should be allowed to show sexually explicit material on the air. (PROBE: Is that strongly or mildly (agree/disagree)?

1999	
6%	Strongly agree
12	Mildly agree

18	Mildly disagree
64	Strongly disagree
1	DK/Ref

d. Thinking specifically about premium/subscription cable channels like HBO, Cinemax, and Showtime, do you think they should be allowed to show sexually explicit material on the air?

1999

25%	Strongly agree
34	Mildly agree
11	Mildly disagree
28	Strongly disagree
2	DK/Ref

e. Basic cable television should be allowed to show sexually explicit material on the air.

1999

10%	Strongly agree
16	Mildly agree
18	Mildly disagree
55	Strongly disagree
1	DK/Ref

f. Television advertisers should be allowed to use sexually explicit material.

1999

4%	Strongly agree
10	Mildly agree
21	Mildly disagree
64	Strongly disagree
–	DK/Ref

g. Print advertisers, in magazines or newspapers, should be allowed to use sexually explicit material.

1999

7%	Strongly agree
16	Mildly agree
20	Mildly disagree
56	Strongly disagree
1	DK/Ref

h. Radio shows should be allowed to discuss sexually explicit material.

1999

10%	Strongly agree
22	Mildly agree
21	Mildly disagree
45	Strongly disagree
1	DK/Ref

    i. Video stores should be allowed to rent sexually explicit videos.

1999

24%	Strongly agree
39	Mildly agree
9	Mildly disagree
25	Strongly disagree
2	DK/Ref

    j. Advertisers should be allowed to place sexually explicit material on billboards.

1999

3%	Strongly agree
6	Mildly agree
15	Mildly disagree
76	Strongly disagree
–	DK/Ref

33. Do you think the federal government should or should not be involved, either directly or indirectly, in requiring the ratings of entertainment television programs?

1999

57%	Should
40	Should not
3	DK/Ref

34. As you may know, the ratings system applies to entertainment shows on TV. Do you think this ratings system should or should not also apply to TV news programs?

1999

59%	Should apply
37	Should not apply
4	DK/Ref

35. There has been a lot of talk lately about rating television programs. Do you think that the government has a role to play in developing a system to rate television programs, or do you think the government should not be involved?

1997

44%	Government should be involved
52	Government should not be involved
4	DK/Ref

36. There has been a lot of talk lately about rating or placing regulations on what is posted on the Internet. Do you think the government has a role to play in developing a system to rate Internet material, or do you think the government should not be involved?

1999

58%	The government should be involved
37	The government should not be involved
4	DK/Ref

37. I'm going to read you some ways people might exercise their First Amendment rights. For each, please tell me if you agree or disagree that someone should be allowed to do it.

   a. Tabloid newspapers such as the *Star* and the *National Enquirer* should have the same freedom to publish what they want as other newspapers such as the *New York Times*, and the *Wall Street Journal*.

1997	1999	
43%	36%	Strongly agree
33	35	Mildly agree
8	8	Mildly disagree
14	19	Strongly disagree
2	2	DK/Ref

   b. Magazines such as *Playboy* and *Hustler* should have the same freedom to publish what they want as other magazines such as *Time* and *Newsweek*.

1999	
39%	Strongly agree
32	Mildly agree
7	Mildly disagree
20	Strongly disagree
2	DK/Ref

   c. Television programs such as "The Jerry Springer Show" and "The Jenny Jones Show" should have the same freedom to air what they want as "ABC News with Peter Jennings."

1999	
30%	Strongly agree
30	Mildly agree
11	Mildly disagree
26	Strongly disagree
3	DK/Ref

38. Please tell me whether you agree or disagree with the following statements.

   a. The press should be allowed to publish factual information that may be embarrassing or sensitive regarding a public official's private life.

1999	
21%	Strongly agree
27	Mildly agree
17	Mildly disagree
34	Strongly disagree
1	DK/Ref

   b. The press should be allowed to publish factual information that may be embarrassing or sensitive regarding a celebrity who has not been voted into a public office.

1999

17%	Strongly agree
27	Mildly agree
22	Mildly disagree
31	Strongly disagree
3	DK/Ref

c. The press should be allowed to publish factual information that may be embarrassing or sensitive regarding an ordinary citizen.

1999

12%	Strongly agree
25	Mildly agree
18	Mildly disagree
42	Strongly disagree
3	DK/Ref

39. Overall, how would you rate the First Amendment's guarantee of freedom of the press in helping the public become informed about issues in government – excellent, good, only fair, or poor?

1997

15%	Excellent
48	Good
28	Only fair
6	Poor
4	DK/Ref

40. Do you think that jailing reporters who refuse to reveal their news sources during a trial is justified when the names are necessary for a fair trial, or is it wrong because people with important information will be afraid to tell the truth to reporters?

1997

36%	Is justified
54	Is wrong
9	DK/Ref

41. Before a criminal case comes to trial, do you think that reporters who have found out about certain facts of the case should be forbidden to publish the information because it might bias jurors, or should they be allowed to publish the information because no one, not even a judge, should be able to censor the press?

1997

51%	Forbidden to publish
42	Allowed to publish
8	DK/Ref

42. Teachers or other public school officials should be allowed to lead prayers in school.

1997	1999	
37%	44%	Strongly agree
20	21	Mildly agree
15	15	Mildly disagree
25	18	Strongly disagree
2	2	DK/Ref

43. Government should be allowed to regulate the activities of celebrity photographers (a.k.a. the paparazzi (PA-PA-RAHT-ZEE)).

1999

29%	Strongly agree
24	Mildly agree
21	Mildly disagree
23	Strongly disagree
4	DK/Ref

44. Please tell me whether you agree or disagree with the following statement: Once the government starts limiting certain rights, it becomes easier for it to put limits on more rights.

64%	Strongly agree
20	Mildly agree
7	Mildly disagree
6	Strongly disagree
3	DK/Ref

a. Do you currently have access to the Internet at work, school, or home?

1999

56%	Yes
44	No
–	DK/Ref

b. Have you used the Internet in the past thirty days?

1999

80%	Yes
20	No
–	DK/Ref

c. On average, how many hours per week do you use the Internet? (Enter two digits.)

Now I'd just like to ask a few questions for classification purposes only.

d. In what year were you born? (Enter two digits: "76" for 1976.)

e. What was the last grade of school you completed? Grade school or less, Some high school, High school, Some college, College grad, Postgraduate.

1999

4%	Grade school or less
13	Some high school

34	High school
1	Trade school
25	Some college
15	College graduate
7	Postgraduate
–	DK/Ref

f. Are you white, black, Hispanic, Asian, or something else?

1999

81%	White
9	Black
4	Hispanic
1	Asian
4	Other (Specify)
1	DK/Ref

g. For classification purposes only, is the total yearly income of all the members of your family now living at home $40,000 or more, or is it less than $40,000?

1999

45%	Under $40,000
48	$40,000 or above
6	DK/Ref

h. And is that . . .

6%	Under $10,000
12	$10,000 to less than $20,000
12	$20,000 to less than $30,000
13	$30,000 to less than $40,000
12	$40,000 to less than $50,000
16	$50,000 to less than $75,000
8	$75,000 to less than $100,000
7	$100,000 or more
4	DK/Ref

i. What is your marital status? Are you, married, divorced, separated, widowed, or have you never been married?

1999

52%	Married
13	Divorced/separated
10	Widowed
24	Never married
1	DK/Ref

j. Are you currently employed full-time, employed part-time, retired, temporarily laid off, or are you not employed?

1999

54%	Employed full-time
11	Employed part-time

18	Retired
3	Temporarily laid off
14	Not employed
–	DK/Ref

k. Are you Catholic, Protestant, Jewish, other Christian, none, or something else?

1999

24%	Catholic
29	Protestant
1	Jewish
22	Other Christian
11	None
10	Something else (specify)
4	DK/Ref

l. Do you attend religious services more than once a week, once a week, two or three times a month, once a month, less than once a month, or not at all?

1999

14%	More than once a week
24	Once a week
11	Two or three times a month
10	Once a month
15	Less than once a month
25	Not at all
1	DK/Ref

m. In politics today, are you a Democrat, a Republican, an independent, or other?

1999

32%	Democrat
26	Republican
24	Independent
12	No preference.
3	Other (vol.)
3	Dk/Ref

n. Politically speaking, do you consider yourself to be liberal, moderate, or conservative?

1999

20%	Liberal
33	Moderate
38	Conservative
2	None (vol.)
7	DK/Ref

o. Do you have any children under the age of eighteen?

1999

39%	Yes
60	No
–	DK/Ref

p. What state do you live in? (Ask for state abbreviation, e.g., CT.)

q. ENTER RESPONDENT'S SEX: (DO NOT ASK).

1999

48%	Male
52	Female

References

PUBLICATIONS

Adamany, David, and Joel B. Grossman. "Support for the Supreme Court as a National Policymaker." *Law and Policy Quarterly* Vol. 5 No. 4 (October, 1983): 405–37.

Anderson, Kristi, and Stuart Thorson. "Public Discourse or Strategic Game? Changes in Our Conception of Elections." *Studies in American Political Development* 3:264 (1989).

Ansolabehere, Stephen, and Shanto Iyengar. *Going Negative*. New York: Free Press, 1995.

Bennett, W. Lance. *Public Opinion in American Politics*. New York: Harcourt Brace Jovanovich, 1980.

Blackstone, Sir William. *Commentaries on the Laws of England*. Dublin: Exshaw et al., 1765.

Blue Engine Corp. (the). "National Survey of Teens on the Internet," conducted by Validata Research LLC, 1999.

Campbell, Angus, Philip E. Converse, Warren E. Miller, and Donald E. Stokes. *The American Voter*. New York: Wiley, 1960.

Chafee, Zecharia. *Free Speech in the United States*. Cambridge, Mass.: Harvard University Press, 1941.

Center for Survey Research and Analysis at the University of Connecticut and First Amendment Center. "Public Opinion about the First Amendment Surveys," 7/97, 3/99, and 9/99.

Converse, Philip E. "The Nature of Belief Systems in Mass Publics," in *Ideology and Discontent*, ed. D. Apter, pp. 206–61. New York: Free Press, 1964.

Dautrich, Kenneth. "The Effects of News Coverage of the Clinton/Lewinsky Story on Public Attitudes of the News Media." A paper delivered at the annual meetings of the American Association for Public Opinion Research, St. Petersburg, Florida, May 1999.

   "The Disconnect Between News Directors and the Public: Explaining Why Americans Are Cynical About the News." A report prepared for the Radio Television News Directors Foundation, June 1999.

Dautrich, Kenneth, and Thomas Hartley. *How the News Media Fail American Voters: Causes, Consequences, and Remedies*. New York: Columbia University Press, 1999.

Davis, Richard, and Diana Owen. *News Media and American Politics*. New York: Oxford University Press, 1998.

de Sola Pool, Ithiel. *Technologies of Freedom*. Cambridge, Mass.: Harvard University Press, 1983.

Delli Carpini, Michael X., and Scott Keeter. *What Americans Know About Politics and Why It Matters*. New Haven, Conn.: Yale University Press, 1996.

Dennis, Jack. *Socialization to Politics*. New York: Wiley, 1973.

Easton, David. *A Systems Analysis of Political Life*. New York: Wiley, 1965.
"A Re-Assessment of the Concept of Political Support." *British Journal of Political Science* 5 (1975): 435–57.

Easton, David, and Jack Dennis, "The Child's Acquisition of Regime Norms: Political Efficacy." *American Political Science Review* 61 (1967): 25–38.
Children in the Political System: Origins of Political Legitimacy. New York: McGraw-Hill, 1969.
"A Political Theory of Political Socialization," in Jack Dennis, ed., *Socialization to Politics: A Reader*. New York: Wiley, 1973.

Epstein, Edward Jay. *Between Fact and Fiction: The Problem with Journalism*. New York: Vintage, 1975.

Erskine, Hazel. "The Polls: Freedom of Speech." *Public Opinion Quarterly* 34 (1970): 483–96.

Freedom Forum and the Roper Center. "American Views of the News: What They Like, What They Don't Like, and What Sources They Use," February 1997.

Friendly, Fred W. *Minnesota Rag*. New York: Random House, 1981.

Grossman, Joel B., and Charles R. Epp. "The Reality of Rights in an Atolerant Society." *The Constitution* (1991): 20–8.

Hallin, Daniel C. "Sound Bite News," in *Blurring the Lines*, ed. Gary R. Orren, New York: Free Press, 1990.

Hofstetter, Richard C. *Bias in the News: Network Television Coverage of the 1972 Election Campaign*. Columbus: Ohio State University Press, 1976.

Hofstetter, Richard C., Mark C. Donovan, Melville R. Klauber, Alexandra Cole, Carolyn J. Huie, and Toshiyuki Yuassa, "Political Talk Radio: A Stereotype Reconsidered." *Political Research Quarterly* 47 (1994): 467–79.

Jamieson, Kathleen Hall. *Dirty Politics: Deception, Distraction and Democracy*. New York: Oxford University Press, 1992.

Jennings, M. Kent, and Richard Niemi. *The Political Character of Adolescents: The Influence of Families and Schools*. Princeton: Princeton University Press, 1974.
Generations and Politics: A Panel Study of Young Adults and Their Parents. Princeton: Princeton University Press, 1981.

Just, Marion R., Ann N. Crigler, Dean E. Alger, Timothy E. Cook, Montague Kern, and Darrell M. West. *Crosstalk: Citizens, Candidates, and the Media in a Presidential Campaign*. Chicago: Chicago University Press, 1996.

Kalven, Harry, Jr. "The New York Times Case: A Note on 'The Central Meaning of the First Amendment.'" *The Supreme Court Review* (1964): 191–221.

Key V. O., Jr. *The Responsible Electorate.* Cambridge, Mass.: Harvard University Press, 1966.

Kurland, Philip, and Ralph Lerner, eds. *The Founders' Constitution.* Chicago: University of Chicago Press, 1987.

Lang, Kurt, and Gladys Lang. *Politics and Television.* Chicago: Quadrangle, 1968.

Leonard, Thomas. *The Power of the Press.* New York: Oxford University Press, 1986.

Levy, Leonard, *Emergence of a Free Press.* New York: Oxford University Press, 1985.

Marcus, George E., et al. *With Malice Toward Some: How People Make Civil Liberties Judgments.* Cambridge: Cambridge University Press, 1995.

Matlin, Jay. "Yes, Americans Still Do Care About the News, But Not the Way They Used To." A paper presented at the annual meetings of the American Association for Public Opinion Research, Norfolk, Virginia, May 1977.

McCloskey, Herbert. "Consensus and Ideology in American Politics." *American Political Science Review*, Vol. 58 (1964): 361–82.

McCloskey, Herbert, and Alida Brill, *Dimensions of Tolerance: What Americans Believe About Civil Liberties.* New York: Russell Sage Foundation, 1983.

McLuhan, Marshall, and Quentin Fiore, *The Medium Is the Message.* New York: Random House, 1967.

Medsger, Betty. *Winds of Change*: Arlington Va.: The Freedom Forum, 1996.

Meiklejohn, Alexander. *Free Speech and Its Relation to Self-Government.* New York: Harper, 1948.

Murphy, Paul. *The Shaping of the First Amendment: 1791 to Present.* New York: Oxford University Press, 1991.

Neuman, W. Russell. *The Paradox of Mass Politics: Knowledge and Opinion in the American Electorate.* Cambridge, Mass.: Harvard University Press, 1986.

The Future of the Mass Audience. New York: Cambridge University Press, 1991.

"Newseum Survey on Trust in the News Media," conducted by The Roper Center for Public Opinion Research, February 1997.

Page, Benjamin I., and Robert Y. Shapiro. *The Rational Public: Fifty Years of Trends in Americans' Policy Preferences.* Chicago: University of Chicago Press, 1992.

Patterson, Thomas C. *Out of Order.* New York: Knopf, 1993.

Pew Center for People and the Press, "A Report on Media Use in the 1996 Election," April 1996.

Popkin, Samuel. *The Reasoning Voter: Communication and Persuasion in Presidential Campaigns.* Chicago: University of Chicago Press, 1991.

Powe, Lucas. *The Fourth Estate and the Constitution: Freedom of the Press in America.* Berkeley: University of California Press, 1991.

Prothro, J., and C. Grigg. "Fundamental Principles of Democracy: Bases of Agreement and Disagreement." *Journal of Politics* 22 (1960): 276–94.

Richards, Robert D. *Freedom's Voice: The Perilous Present and Uncertain Future of the First Amendment*. New York: Brassey's, Inc., 1998.

Robinson, Michael J., and Margaret A. Sheehan. *Over the Wire and on TV: CBS and UPI in Campaign '80*. New York: Russell Sage Foundation, 1983.

Sabato, Larry. *Feeding Frenzy: How Attack Journalism Has Transformed American Politics*. New York: Free Press, 1993.

Sanford, Bruce W. *Don't Shoot the Messenger: How Our Growing Hatred of the Media Threatens Free Speech for All of Us*. New York: Free Press, 1999.

Sarat, Austin, "Studying American Legal Culture: An Assessment of Survey Evidence." *Law and Society* 11 (Winter, 1997): 427–88.

Schudson, Michael. *The Power of the News*. Cambridge, Mass.: Harvard University Press, 1995.

Schwartz, David C., and Sandra Kenyon. *New Directions in Political Socialization*. New York: Free Press, 1975.

Shafer, Byron E., and William J. M. Clagget. *The Two Majorities*. Baltimore: Johns Hopkins University Press, 1995.

Smolla, Rod. *Deliberate Intent: A Lawyer Tells the True Story of Murder by the Book*. New York: Crown Publishers, 1999.

Stevenson, Robert L., and Mark T. Greene, "A Reconsideration of Bias in the News." *Journalism Quarterly* 57 (1980): 115–21.

Stouffer, Samuel. *Communism, Conformity and Civil Liberties*. New York: Doubleday, 1955.

Sullivan, John L., George E. Marcus, James E. Pierson, and Stanley Feldman. "The Development of Political Tolerance: The Impact of Social Class, Personality and Cognition." *International Journal of Political Education* 2 (1978–9): 115–39.

Taylor, Paul. *See How They Run: Electing a President in an Age of Mediaocracy*. New York: Knopf, 1990.

Tribe, Laurence H. *American Constitutional Law, second edition*. New York: Foundation Press, 1988.

Weaver, Paul H. "Is Television News Biased?" *Public Interest* (Winter) 26 (1972): 57–74.

"Work Trends: Uses of Technology in the Workplace." A study conducted by the Center for Survey Research and Analysis at University of Connecticut and the Heldrich Center at Rutgers University, 1999.

Yankelovich, Daniel. *Coming to Public Judgement*. New York: Syracuse University Press, 1991.

Zaller, John R. *The Nature and Origin of Mass Opinion*. New York: Cambridge University Press, 1992.

COURT CASES CITED

Ashcroft v. ACLU, Case No. 00–1293 (U.S. Sup. Ct.).

Brandenburg v. Ohio, 395 U.S. 444 (1969)

Chaplinsky v. State of New Hampshire, 315 U.S. 568 (1942)

City of Boerne v. Flores, 521 U.S. 507 (1997)

Clark v. Community for Creative Non-Violence, 468 U.S. 288 (1984)

FCC v. Pacifica Foundation, 438 U.S. 726 (1978)

Food Lion, Inc. v. Capitol Cities/ABC, Inc., 194 F.3d 505 (4th Cir. 1999)

Heffron v. International Society for Krishna Consciousness, 452 U.S. 640 (1981)

Home Box Office, Inc. v. F.C.C., 567 F.2d 9 (D.C. Cir. 1977)

Jacobellis v. State of Ohio, 378 U.S. 184 (1964)

Miami Herald Publishing Co. v. Tornillo, 418 U.S. 241 (1974)

National Broadcasting Co. v. United States, 319 U.S. 190 (1943)

Near v. State of Minnesota Ex. Rel. Olson, 283 U.S. 697 (1931)

New York Times Co. v. United States, 403 U.S. 713 (1971)

New York Times Co. v. Sullivan, 376 U.S. 254 (1964)

Red Lion Broadcasting Co. v. F.C.C., 395 U.S. 367 (1969)

Reno v. American Civil Liberties Union, 521 U.S. 844 (1997)

Texas v. Johnson, 491 U.S. 397 (1989)

Ward v. Rock Against Racism, 491 U.S. 781 (1989)

Wilkinson v. Jones, 480 U.S. 926 (1987)

Wisconsin v. Mitchell, 508 U.S. 476 (1993)

Wooley v. Maynard, 430 U.S. 705 (1977)

Index